Centurion

Empress of Death

An Artorian Novella

James Mace

Electronic Edition Copyright © 2017 by James Mace

All rights reserved as permitted under the U.S. Copyright Act of 1976, no part of this publication may be reproduced, distributed, or transmitted in any form or by any means, or stored in a database or retrieval system, without the prior permission of the publisher.

Characters and events portrayed in this book are based on actual persons and events, but are used fictitiously.

Legionary Books
Meridian, Idaho 83642, USA
http://www.legionarybooks.net

First eBook Edition: 2011

Published in the United States of America
Legionary Books

Cover Image, *The Death of Valeria Messalina*, by Victor Biennoury (mid 19th century), public domain as of December 1993

All other images are licensed through applicable copyright holders, or public domain

She takes away all of your fears and pain
Brings on death, takes your soul to the nothingness
Queen of the night will bring eternal dark
Here she comes, Goddess of Death!

- Crystal Viper, *Goddess of Death*

The Works of James Mace

Note: In each series or combination of series', all works are listed in chronological sequence

The Artorian Chronicles
Soldier of Rome: The Legionary
Soldier of Rome: The Sacrovir Revolt
Soldier of Rome: Heir to Rebellion
Soldier of Rome: The Centurion
*Empire Betrayed: The Fall of Sejanus
Soldier of Rome: Journey to Judea
Soldier of Rome: The Last Campaign

*Centurion Valens and the Empress of Death
*Slaves of Fear: A Land Unconquered

The Great Jewish Revolt and Year of the Four Emperors
Soldier of Rome: Rebellion in Judea
Soldier of Rome: Vespasian's Fury
Soldier of Rome: Reign of the Tyrants
Soldier of Rome: Rise of the Flavians
Soldier of Rome: The Fall of Jerusalem

Napoleonic Era
Forlorn Hope: The Storming of Badajoz
I Stood With Wellington
Courage, Marshal Ney

The Anglo-Zulu War
Brutal Valour: The Tragedy of Isandlwana
Crucible of Honour: The Battle of Rorke's Drift

* Stand-alone novel or novella

Table of Contents

The Character of Centurion Tiberius Valens
Preface
Cast of Characters
Chapter I: End of the Journey
Chapter II: Agony and Ecstasy
Chapter III: An Uneasy Return
Chapter IV: Shadows of Intrigue
Chapter V: The Last Triumph
Chapter VI: Web of Deceit
Chapter VII: Empress of Lust
Chapter VIII: Empress of Death
Chapter IX: A Thief's Punishment
Chapter X: Imperial Treachery
Chapter XI: Lost and Redeemed
Epilogue: Four Years Later
Historical Postscript

The Character of Centurion Tiberius Valens

Many times when we are inspired to write a story, there is not enough to warrant an entire book, or perhaps we wish to write about a character from an existing series who is someone other than the main protagonist. Stephen King wrote an entire series of novellas that, even though they were far shorter than his usual books, were still very well received. Three in particular, *The Body*, *Rita Hayworth and the Shawshank Redemption*, and *The Green Mile*, were made into highly successful films.

The motivation behind this story came from the character of Tiberius Valens, from my series, *The Artorian Chronicles*, He was meant to be used one time for comic effect when I wrote my first book, *Soldier of Rome: The Legionary*, back in 2004 to 2005. As I was still new to writing, many of the cast were rather one-dimensional during this time, and having a sexually prolific character, with absolutely no sense of shame, added a level of humour to what is otherwise a very dark and brutal story.

Valens returned in the second book, *The Sacrovir Revolt*, though his role changed very little. I was still very focused on developing the characters of Artorius and Magnus, and I did not ever foresee Valens becoming an integral part of the story. That changed inadvertently when I was writing the third book, *Heir to Rebellion*. During the scenes involving, Erin, the slave girl, as well as the child that would become her adopted son, I needed a legionary involved in this part of the plot. I picked Valens' name completely at random. Suddenly that arc of the story, combined with Valens' semi-humorous courting of Magnus' sister, Svetlana, added depth and human interest to his character. By the time I wrote book four, *The Centurion*, Valens had become a 'break out character' within the series; with many fans listing both him and Vitruvius among their favourites.

At this point I realized Valens had enough personality to warrant his own story. I envisioned a rather torrid saga involving him transgressing with the infamous Valeria Messalina, Empress Consort from 41 to 48 A.D. This places things in an unusual position when looking at the timelines of the story. *Empress of Death* takes place in 44 A.D., yet at the time of writing it, the series had only progressed as far as 28 A.D. With this novella, the reader gets a bit of a glimpse at what happens to some of the characters much later. One observation that fans of the series will note right away is that, while this novella is considered part of the Artorian canon, Artorius himself is completely absent. He is mentioned in passing while recapping events from earlier books of the series. My reasons for this were two-fold. First, it is Valens' story, not Artorius', and I did not want Valens to get overshadowed. The second reason is that, since this novella came out before books five and six of *The Artorian Chronicles*, one is left wondering about the fate of Artorius. We assume that he takes part in the Invasion of Britain, since Valens has just returned from there. However, since he is not in this story, the reader is left guessing whether that means he is killed in the final book. To get that answer, one will just have to wait until the final two books of the series are complete.

With all these things in mind, the reader still gets a glimpse into the future and Valens gets his own story. I hope it is one that fans of *The Artorian Chronicles*, as well as new readers can all enjoy.

James Mace – October 2011

Preface

In the year 44 A.D., following the Conquest of Britannia, Centurion Tiberius Valens returns to Rome in Triumph. It will be his last official act as a soldier of the Empire, as he looks forward to a well-deserved retirement. Instead, a night of drunken debauchery leads him into a web of deceit, betrayal, and unholy lust. Valens tries to salvage his sanity and his life as he plunges further down a harrowing decent into madness, wrought by the hands of the Empress Messalina herself.

Cast of Characters

Tiberius Valens – A Centurion readying to retire from the Twentieth Legion
Gaius Praxus – A Centurion Primus Ordo within the Twentieth Legion and a friend of Valens
Svetlana Flaviana – Valens' wife
Cornelius – A Praetorian Centurion who served with Valens in Judea
Oleg Flavianus – Svetlana's brother

Noble Romans:
Claudius Drusus Caesar – Emperor of Rome
Valeria Messalina – Claudius' third wife, Empress of Rome
Claudia Antonia – Daughter of Claudius from his second wife, Aelia Paetina
Gnaeus Pompey Magnus – Husband of Antonia and descendant of the famous Triumvir of the same name

Chapter I: End of the Journey
Rome, May, 44 A.D.

Emperor Claudius

The journey was finally at an end; the port of Ostia came into sight, eliciting a raucous cheer from the mass of legionaries who had been living on the deck of the chartered merchant ship for the past two weeks. More than ten thousand soldiers of Rome were bound for the Eternal City on a fleet of rotting hulks carrying all sorts of nefarious cargo to the far corners of the Empire. Ostia was the main port for Rome, the heart and light of the civilized world. It was also where the first triumphal celebration in a generation was about to begin, following the conquest of Britannia the previous year.

For Centurion Tiberius Valens, it was the end of an even longer journey. His service to Rome had lasted for more than three decades and it was time to bring his career to an end. He would march in the triumphal parade at the head of his legionaries in his last official act as a soldier of the Empire. He leaned on the rail, feeling the spray of salt water against his body as the ship rose and fell in the ocean swell. Though Ostia was in sight, its closeness was deceiving; it would be several hours before they docked.

"I've been doing this for far too long," he said quietly to himself.

"Sir?" a nearby legionary asked. Valens shook his head and the soldier left him to his reminiscing. In many ways, the life of a legionary kept a Roman man far younger than his contemporaries. It was the only profession a Plebeian could enter where he had a guaranteed source of income, a steady diet, and enforced personal hygiene and cleanliness. The constant marching and physical training kept a legionary fit long past the age when most bodies would start to decline into poor health.

It all came with a terrible price. Valens' body bore the scars of many adversaries and though he was far more physically fit than most men his age, his body ached constantly. The emotional scars within-the ones that you never talked about publicly-were the ones that ran the deepest. A soldier's life was not one of constant battles, yet battles did happen. Valens had fought in numerous wars in Germania, Gaul, Frisia, and Judea. Two of his closest friends had died in Frisia at the Battle of Braduhenna; which was perhaps the closest run battle Valens had ever taken part in. Braduhenna had happened sixteen years before, yet still in the night he would often find himself awaken with nightmares of that dark forest with his friends crying out to him as they died in terrible agony. No matter how one-sided a battle was, Roman soldiers still died.

The Invasion of Britannia had been no different. The Britons, though exceptionally brave and well armed, were devoid of body armour, and lacked any type of cohesion or discipline. The Roman ability to coordinate attacks, individual discipline on the battle line, and far superior weaponry, ensured that each battle was a terrible mismatch. Yet even when they knew they could not win, they still fought with extreme tenacity, making every Roman victory a costly one. They had fought to protect their lands and people from conquest, and Valens could not help but admire their fanatical bravery.

He leaned on the rail and breathed deeply as the ship lurched forward, the salt water spraying his face once more. The sun was starting to fall behind them in the west as the ship lurched slowly towards the harbour. Standing on the prow was another old friend of his, Centurion Primus Ordo Gaius Praxus. Praxus had served in the legions even longer than Valens; and the two had followed each other from one corner of the Empire to the other.

"It is the end of an era for us," Valens said as he leaned against the rail.

"We've made a good run of it," Praxus replied. "It is time we passed our swords to the next generation." He too had submitted his request for retirement. His wife, Alane, had come from a wealthy merchant family and Praxus had amassed his own fortune over the decades of his career. His son was now a legionary and the two had served together in Britannia. For Praxus, being able to pass the sword on to his son signified that it was time for him to leave the ranks. He had done this literally; following the fall of the final stronghold held by the Catuvellauni, Praxus handed his still-bloodied gladius to his son, Ioan.

The sight of the harbour gave a false sense of distance and it still took a couple of hours for the ship to finally dock in the crowded harbour. This brought about a second round of cheers from the host of legionaries who fought to get past each other and off the ship. They were given a few days of leave before they had to report to the local barracks. After the month-long Triumphal celebrations came to an end, most of them would head back to Britannia and take part in the continued pacification of the province.

"You know I don't really belong here," Valens said quietly. Praxus snorted in reply.

"Who among us does?" he observed. "We've spent our lives on the frontier, in the darkest corners of the world that the patricians either pretend does not exist, or they build monuments of marble to denote their conquests."

"It is a strange paradox," Valens remarked. "We bring peace, order, and light to the darkness at the point of the sword because there is no other way. Those who pretend that the uncivilized only want to live in peace have never seen an altar with smouldering remains from a human sacrifice, or the disembowelled corpses of women and children that were defiled before they were killed. Yet what happens to those who bring the light? Where do we go when Rome no longer has any use for us?"

"That is the one thing they never really plan for," his friend replied. "Oh they give us a pension and send us on our way; far better than a spent warrior from Britannia or Parthia. However, they don't *really* know what to do with us. I think they give our men plots of land in veterans' colonies because they know deep down that our lads are never really fit to be a part of civilized society."

"And those of us who have supposedly risen above that?" Valens' question was directed towards soldiers of the Centurionate. Those minute few who ever rose to the rank of Centurion or above joined the *equites*, the order of lesser nobility that would place them above the common plebeians and just below the senatorial patricians.

"We could run for public office, I suppose," Praxus conjectured. Valens scoffed at the notion.

"The only office I'd be fit to hold is in a local brothel, determining which whores are so badly infected they cannot still be of use."

"I think they have something like that under the health and public sanitation magistracy," Praxus said, giving both men a short laugh. Valens let out a long sigh.

"No," he said after a brief pause. "In my heart I will always be a soldier of Rome, but I cannot stay here." Praxus nodded in understanding, for they had shared many such conversations like these over the decades.

Valens longed to head north, to the ancestral homeland of his wife, Svetlana. Her grandfather, Olaf, had been a Nordic nobleman who had served as an auxiliary in the Roman Army, thereby earning the family Roman citizenship. Two of Svetlana's brothers had also served in the Roman military; Hansi as a sailor, and Magnus as a soldier. Magnus and Valens were in the same squad many years ago, when both were young legionaries. His Nordic friend had risen quickly through the ranks, achieving the position of Centurion Primus Ordo; the second highest rank a common soldier could ever attain.

His thoughts were brought back to the present as the ship heaved to with an audible crash into the side of the dock.

"Here we are then!" Praxus said as he steadied himself on the railing. He was scanning the throng of people that had mixed in with the usual chaos of the pier.

"A pity Ioan could not come with you," Valens replied as legionaries hefted their packs and scrambled to the ramp that led down to the docks.

"Britannia is far from pacified, regardless of what the Emperor thinks," Praxus observed. "I passed my sword on to him, like he will do in years to come when he has his own sons. But for now, it is his time to keep the Empire safe. Ah, there's Alane." Without another word, he bolted for the plank, waving to his wife as he did so.

Unlike most of the soldiers, Valens took his time disembarking. Svetlana was traveling by land from the border territory near the Nordic realms and would not be in Rome for a few more days at least, depending on when she had started her journey. Valens watched as Praxus leapt off the ship and raced into the waiting arms of his wife. Valens smiled and sighed.

He elected to stay in Ostia with his wife's family rather than in Rome. Svetlana's brother, Hansi, had recently returned to the northlands, having served out an honourable career in the Roman Navy. He had commanded his own ship during the Invasion of Britannia. This had involved him staying on longer than he'd anticipated; however, he had done so in part because he understood the historical significance of what they were undertaking. It had been as a favour to his commander, Admiral Stoppello, who had been the same naval officer to take Valens and his friends to Judea thirteen years prior.

Svetlana's grandfather, Olaf, had finally passed away at the extremely advanced age of one hundred and three. He had already been an overlord with sizeable lands when he joined the Roman Army, and his years in the ranks as an Auxiliary Centurion had enriched his coffers. Since the oldest of the grandsons, Oleg, had decided to remain in Rome, Hansi had taken it upon himself to lord over their grandfather's lands. Svetlana had remained there until her brother arrived.

Valens did not have a sense of homeland like his wife and her family did. He was born in a Roman fortress to a legionary father and a woman of unknown origins. His parents had both passed into the afterlife within a couple years of Valens following his father into the legions. It was regrettable that his mother never delved into her origins, and his father would only say about their lineage was, "You are a Roman and that is good enough."

As he finally disembarked, the crowds on the docks were starting to disperse. Officers with families had left with, with most of the legionaries running off with the bevy of anxious whores who were ready to pleasure their collective manhood at the cost of a few denarii and the risk of exotic diseases. As he made his way towards the town itself, Valens realized that this was only the third time to the Eternal City that he had spent so much of his life fighting for. His home had been wherever the Legions had required him. He had grown up in North Africa and Spain, where his father was posted, yet most of his own career had been spent on the Rhine in Germania. This was interrupted by a six-year stint in the unbearable heat of Judea. He would return to Germania for a few years before taking part in the Invasion of Britannia. Yet while his Legion, the Twentieth Valeria, would remain in the newly conquered Isle, he was headed for different shores.

Chapter II: Agony and Ecstasy

Empress Valeria Messalina

The sun had set by the time Valens reached the house of his wife's family. It felt almost deserted. Svetlana's father, Svend, had passed on two years before his own father. Olaf once told Valens that the greatest tragedy in his life was that he outlived all three of his sons, of whom Svend was the only one to have children. Of these, Hansi had travelled straight to his grandfather's Nordic realms, rather than return to Rome. Oleg had his own house in Rome, where he lived with his wife and daughters. He saw to it that their father's home was maintained by a handful of slaves, should Magnus wish to claim it for his own when he returned from Britannia in another year.

"Master, you've returned," Erin said as Valens walked through the entranceway. She bowed deeply before him and immediately started collecting his belongings. In truth, Valens was fond of the slave woman. How he had acquired her was an unusual story; but then, such had been his entire life, he reckoned.

She had been an unwilling participant in a minor slave rebellion in Gaul more than twenty years before. Valens thought back to that day in the city of Lugdunum. He was still but a legionary in the ranks then. In the ensuing skirmish within the confines of an alleyway, Valens had unknowingly killed Erin's young husband, who had been trying to protect her from the onslaught of legionaries. Valens had even smashed Erin across the head with the boss of his shield during the brawl, yet in a rare act of mercy he elected not to kill her. He would later explain it was because she was unarmed, but the truth was he had no idea why he spared her. In conflicts before and since, he had willingly slain men and women, whether they were armed or unarmed. When the survivors were sold back into slavery, he had felt obligated to purchase her. At that time, Erin could not speak Latin, but Svetlana spoke Gallic and she had taken to the young slave immediately.

"Master, I hoped you would have word about my son," Erin remarked as she carried Valens' kit to the guest quarters. During another slave rebellion that had occurred soon after he had acquired Erin, they had been ordered to give no quarter, rather than attempt to sell the survivors back into slavery. Following a skirmish, Valens saw his squad leader, Artorius, about to kill a new-born child whose parents they had just crucified. In another baffling act of clemency, he instead compelled Artorius to let him take the child, which he then gave to Erin to raise as her own. That new-born baby, who Erin had named Tynan, was now in his twenties. Valens had given him his freedom several years before, and the young man had enlisted into the Roman auxilia. He had acquitted himself well enough in battle. Provided he lived through the next twenty-five years, he would become a Roman citizen. Valens reckoned this was a decent fate for one who had been born a slave and had almost died by the sword before he was a month old.

"He is doing well," the Centurion replied, "though he was wounded at the river battle." Erin stopped in her tracks and gasped. She had not seen her son in over a year and had heard no word from him.

"Not badly hurt, is he?" she asked, her eyes pleading. Valens shook his head.

"No," he replied. "He made a full recovery and is now stationed with his unit as part of a garrison requested by our ally, Queen Cartimandua." It had been a good posting for Tynan.

"I am glad to hear he has done well," Erin said quietly. "I also cannot thank you enough for granting him his freedom. He can now become a Roman citizen like you."

"Yes," Valens agreed. It was unusual for one to talk so informally with a slave, yet Erin had been in his service for so long and lived in such intimate quarters with both Valens and Svetlana, that she did not seem like a piece of property. Svetlana was indeed very fond of Erin and the two were practically inseparable at times.

"Once we have my personal belongs stowed, you will accompany me down to the docks to help retrieve the rest of my baggage," Valens directed.

"Of course, master," Erin replied.

The first two days passed uneventfully. Officers were granted leave as well as their men. The real reason for this show of generosity was that one of the heroes of the invasion, Flavius Vespasian, was still en route back to Rome.

On the second evening, Valens was walking back from the docks when he saw a group of men walking towards him. There was a stumble to their step and they were singing a rather rude song about an Arcadian whore who had given them all an unnamed, yet apparently amusing infection.

"Oy! There's the Centurion!" one of the men shouted. He waved excitedly at Valens, who could only smile and wave back.

"Go on home, I may be late," he told Erin, who bowed in reply.

"You didn't think we'd let you get away that easily, did you sir?" one of the men said with a slight slur as he thrust a wine jug into Valens' face.

"Come on lads, you know I don't really drink," he replied, trying to push the pungent jug away from him. "And why couldn't you have at least splurged on some quality vintage? That reeks of vinegar and mare sweat!"

"Need all the coin we can get if we're going to get some quality twat," another soldier remarked with a boisterous laugh, followed by a vile smelling belch. The poor fellow had his arms around two of his friends and looked like he may not stay conscious long enough to find suitable female companionship. Valens let out a sigh and shook his head. He then started laughing. It had been too long since he'd allowed himself to enjoy the frivolous pleasures of a ranker.

"Here, let's get rid of that fermented piss!" He snatched the jug away and threw it with a hard crash onto the cobblestones. "We will have only the best spirits for my men; the conquerors of Britannia!" This elicited a voracious cheer from his men.

The last time Rome had celebrated a triumph of this magnitude had been twenty-seven years before, after the defeat of Arminius and the Germanic Alliance. Even after all these years, Valens still remembered the tavern. It overlooked the Tiber River, with a large stone patio and a warm breeze that blew in off the water. He chuckled to himself as he remembered a particular night before the triumphal parades where he had ran naked down the slope to the river; a pair of fetching young ladies in tow. He then sighed as he realized that not one of the men who accompanied him this night was in the army during that time. In fact, a good number of his soldiers had not even been born yet! Still, here they were in a very familiar setting to the Centurion; in a high state of inebriation and desperate to fuck any young woman willing to do what they deemed was her patriotic duty to the conquerors of Britannia. The women who were fawning over his soldiers bore a striking resemblance to the same ones who had taken care of Valens and his friends all those years ago. For all he knew, they were the daughters of those very same ladies of the night!

"As long as I'm not their father," he chuckled quietly to himself.

Valens was beginning to regret allowing his men to take him out to the taverns. He had never been much of a drinker, even in his younger days. Though he appreciated the old memories that would meld with new ones, his vision was starting to blur and he had trouble standing. The legionaries who had insisted on his joining them now appeared to have an equal or greater number of willing harlots clinging to them.

"Hey, the Centurion doesn't have one yet!" one of the men shouted, pointing to the companionless Valens.

"Here sir, you want one of mine?" another one asked, who had a pair of scantily clad whores sitting on his lap. He slapped one hard on the butt. "You want this one? She swears she can suck your balls straight through the head of your cock!"

"I can get my own, thank you!" Valens retorted, stumbling to his feet to the cheers of his men. It had been years since he had had to acquire his own whores. Svetlana would often do this for him, carefully selecting only the highest quality in supple flesh that she would first sample for herself before sharing with her husband. Still, it should not be that difficult, he reasoned through his clouding mind. After all, he was a Centurion! He had led men in the conquest of many nations and as such, the women of Rome *owed* it to the valiant hero to suck on his cock! And if patriotism wasn't enough…well he had plenty of money. The men started into another rousing chorus about the mysterious Arcadian whore as Valens stumbled off to find a brothel. In his dulled senses, he failed to realize that he had no idea where the nearest house of pleasure was, and before too long he had no idea where he was.

The effects of alcohol were growing worse, despite his not having had a drink in nearly an hour. Whatever it was his men had forced down his gullet, it was wreaking havoc on his senses. He stumbled down an alleyway and leaned against the wall as he started to vomit uncontrollably. He spewed up copious amounts of vile liquid and continued to retch for a minute even after there was nothing left.

"There…that's better," he slurred, wiping his mouth off on his forearm. He was suddenly grossed out by what he had done and he looked around to find someplace to wipe his forearm off. He grinned when he saw a homeless vagrant lying in the gutter. Whether the man was passed out or dead did not matter, he had a soiled blanket covering him that the Centurion used to wipe his arm off.

"Okay you sultry bitches, where are you hiding?" he asked the empty alley. He staggered through the empty back streets that were so cramped that the air was stagnant and they never saw the light of day. In the back of his mind, he tried to come to grips with the fact that he was completely lost.

"Hope I don't get mugged before I can offload a couple denarii and my swollen loins."

The sound of boisterous laughter caught his attention. It was coming from the far end of the alley and a grin came to Valens' face as he stumbled towards the sounds of merriment. A bright light came up a short flight of stairs that led down to a basement doorway. There was no actual door, only a set of brightly coloured curtains. A number of the voices coming from within sounded female, which was all Valens needed to hear and he practically fell through the curtains. A pair of rather large bodyguards stood on either side, and they immediately grabbed a hold of him.

"Hey sorry fellas, but I'm not your type!" Valens said with a laugh.

"This is a *private* party!" one of the burly men growled. Even through his blurry vision, Valens recognized how the men were dressed. These were not street thugs paid to bully unruly patrons, they were Praetorian Guardsmen!

"What the bloody hell are you lot doing here, and in uniform?" Valens asked. "Trying to take all the nice ones for yourselves, are you? You pompous twats!" One of them men raised a fist to smash him in the face when he was restrained by a woman's voice.

"It's alright, let him in." Through the lamplights and haze of opium smoke, he could not make out the face behind the voice, but Valens was suddenly grateful.

"Well what have we here?" another woman asked, eyeing his red tunic and decorated leather belt that betrayed his identity. "Why it's a legionary!"

"*Centurion*, thank you very much!" Valens corrected as he loosed himself from the Praetorian's grip. The second guardsman grabbed him by the shoulder.

"Valens, what the fuck are you doing here?" He recognized the voice and was surprised when he turned to face the man.

"Shit, Cornelius! I should ask you the same thing." Cornelius had served as a Centurion with him in Judea, when Valens was still an Optio. He had taken a position with the Praetorians after their return and that was the last he had seen of him. Though his mind was still fighting the effects of inebriation, Valens comprehended that something was amiss for Cornelius to be here while apparently on duty.

"Old friends, are we?" the first woman's voice asked through the haze.

"More or less," Valens replied.

"You should not be here," Cornelius said quietly. "You have no idea what you've stepped into. Leave now, while you can!"

"I'm not going anywhere until one of these strumpets has relieved me of the excess load swelling in my balls!" Valens retorted. He then felt a much softer pair of hands on his shoulders.

"And no reason for you to leave us, not now," the first woman's voice said seductively into his ear. She then addressed the Praetorians. "Thank you, Cornelius. That will be all."

Cornelius released his grip on Valens, bowed deeply, and stepped away. With a grin of triumph, Valens turned to face his saviour. She was of similar height to him, with shoulder length auburn hair and piercing eyes. Somehow, he knew he would never forget that gaze. She was young, perhaps in her early twenties, with average sized breasts and a very firm body.

"Yes," she said as she apprised him. "He'll do. I have yet to have one of the returning conquerors. You'd best be able to work me over as well as you did those uncivilized barbarians!"

"My 'sword' is at your disposal," Valens replied as she led him through another set of curtains to a back room. There was an elevated long couch in the centre. The walls were lined with both men and women in various stages of undress. His hostess dropped her stola and lay on the couch on her side. Her body was enticing and he was extremely aroused.

"So, are they going to participate or just watch?" he asked, pointing to the people who stood silently watching, their faces rapt with lust.

"Whatever I tell them to do," the woman replied. She then waved him over with her finger. He pulled off his tunic and made ready to fall on top of her. She abruptly sat up, grabbed him by the hair with both hands, and forced his face between her legs.

"Oh no," she purred, "You have to get me warmed up first."

Valens was surprised by the young woman's strength, but was only too happy to oblige as he felt the heat radiating from inside her as he worked her over with his tongue. She kept a hard grip on his hair and started to grind her hips into his face. Soon she was shrieking in ecstasy and thrashing about violently. Without warning, she jerked hard on his hair and pulled him on top of her. She wrapped her strong legs around his waist as he entered her. He marvelled at how incredibly tight she was as he thrust inside of her hard and fast. He became oblivious to the crowd that watched with lustful glee and were now starting to toy with each other as their mistress groaned loudly under the powerful assault of the Centurion. She bit him hard on the neck and raked her fingernails across his back.

His body was partially numb and he could feel a trickle of blood from where she had torn into his flesh. She whispered into his ear words which he could not comprehend. He wasn't sure if this was due to his intoxication or if she was chanting unholy verses in a foreign tongue:

Me olc bris agat!
Ta sibh mo cheannsa!
Sciuirse cara duinn an ithir!
Me fein do anam! Me fein do anam!

Her chants had a sinister air to them, and the final stanza became louder as she repeated it again and again, *"Me fein do anam! Me fein do anam!"* A shiver ran up his spine as her sinister chant echoed in his mind. Through the haze of incense and opiate smoke he could just make out the dark expression on her face. Her eyes grew black as she let loose a howl of demonic ecstasy. This sent him over the edge and he erupted with a torrent of pent up lust and fury. As his lover rolled him off of her, she gave him a chalice, which he thirstily drank from. His mind almost immediately clouded and he faded into darkness to the sounds of malicious laughter.

"What shall we do with him?" a voice asked in the darkness.

"Leave him," the woman replied. "He will return to me soon enough."

Chapter III: An Uneasy Return

A variety of tokens used in Roman brothels

Valens had no idea what time it was as it was now completely dark inside the brothel. His companion had gone; in fact, the place was completely deserted. As he stumbled about in the dark searching for his clothes, he found his money purse and was surprised to find that he had not been robbed. He breathed a sigh of relief and thanked whatever gods happened to be listening.

The predawn was casting its glow as he stumbled up the stairs. His head throbbed and he wanted to get back home and rest. There was a feast planned at the imperial palace that night, and all visiting soldiers holding the rank of Centurion or above were expected to attend. It would probably be as close as he would ever come to meeting the Emperor, which was an opportunity best not squandered.

He still had no idea where he was and he wandered along aimlessly for a while. There were but a few people about and they paid him no mind. He knew he was in a wicked part of the city and that the sooner he was gone, the better. Luckily for him, the gang lords who ruled over the slums had told their men to leave be any soldiers who got lost in their territory. The government allowed them a lot of leeway, seeing as how they kept the dregs under control. The few coins that could be had from mugging or murdering a lost legionary were not worth the risk of losing that autonomy and bringing down the Emperor's wrath. Those who had neglected to appreciate imperial magnanimity in the past had seen their dens ransacked by the Praetorians, and their disembowelled corpses left floating in the Tiber.

Valens' stomach gnawed at him. He had not eaten since the previous evening, and most of that had been expelled from his gut during his retching fit. He was still nauseated and knew he needed to eat. He passed a fruit vendor, yet he was afraid of eating anything in this contaminated part of the city. The sights of vagrants sleeping in the gutters, piles of rotten food and human waste, all reminded him that this was a very dark corner of the Imperial City. Everyone knew it existed, but no one ever wished to discuss it.

The sound of the river caught his attention and he walked briskly towards it. Just past a warehouse he welcomed the sight of the Tiber. While still fully dressed, he stepped out into the slow-moving current. He then submerged himself vigorously into the cold water, letting it bite into his flesh, invigorating him and washing away the contagion of the night before. A few early risers watched with amusement as the Centurion hooted and shouted with renewed energy as he splashed about. His perpetual grin returned, he casually walked out of the river and strolled along the bank, trying to find something that looked familiar to him as the water dripped from his tunic and squished from his sandals. He was relieved to see the veranda of the tavern from the night before.

"Bloody hell, how far did I walk last night?" he mused to himself. "Valens, you really got yourself lost! Oh well, no harm done then."

With wheeled traffic prohibited during the day, he wasn't able to get any kind of transport back to Ostia until he had walked some miles to the edge of the city. A single denarius had bought him a ride in the back of a hay wagon, where he dozed while cursing every rut in the road that renewed his simmering headache. It was late morning when he reached home. Only a few servants appeared to be up and about, and he quietly made his way into the guest quarters. He was about to pull off his still damp tunic when the door was slammed open.

"There you are!" a woman's voice shouted. Valens forced a weak smile as he laid eyes on his wife for the first time in over a year. It was not the type of reunion he had envisioned, though he quickly took her in his arms and kissed her passionately. She kissed him back with equal vigour.

"I didn't expect to see you yet," Valens said as he held Svetlana close; a feeling of relief washing over him.

"I rode all night," Svetlana explained. "Erin said your men had taken you out to celebrate."

"I'm sorry, my love," Valens replied, feeling incredibly guilty. "If I had known…" Svetlana placed a finger over his lips, quieting him. Valens stepped back and removed his damp tunic. As he turned away for a moment, Svetlana's eyes grew wide.

"What the hell is *that?*" she shouted, pointing to his back, which was scored with claw marks from his previous night's companion. "You've been off fucking the little tramps without me!" She smacked him hard across the face, causing his subsiding headache to come back with a vengeance.

"I would have waited for you, had I known you were going to be here!" Valens retorted, grabbing his throbbing head in his hands.

"She wasn't some disgusting, toothless whore I hope!"

"No, she was actually…quite stunning." His words caused Svetlana to smack him again.

"Well you'd better take me to her so that I can have some of her too, then!"

"I would if I could remember where I was," Valens replied. "The lads got me so wasted I have no idea how I found the place to begin with."

"Well you'd better start remembering!" Svetlana retorted, smacking him hard a third time. Valens finally lost his temper and responded with a hard blow from the palm of his hand across her face. Svetlana was a strong, Nordic woman, who was tougher than most men. Her beauty hid this from all but those who were closest to her.

"That's what I've been waiting for!" she responded with a wicked grin, which Valens returned. He then summoned up his strength, grabbed her hard by the throat, and slammed her onto the bed. He roughly tore her clothes off and proceeded to kiss her passionately. She bit him hard on the neck, causing him to grab her hard by the throat once more as he thrust his raging hard member inside her. She grabbed his hand and pulled it harder into her throat, goading him to choke her harder.

"Fuck…fuck…fuck!" she growled as he slammed into her repeatedly. His strength was renewed in the wave of desire brought on by his wife. His body felt rejuvenated as Svetlana grinded her hips into him, goading him on. She then stopped him and shoved him off her, onto his back.

"Wait, I've got a little something extra for you," she said as she kissed him gently. She opened the door and Erin walked in, wearing nothing but a translucent robe. Valens smiled as he had fond memories from over the years when he and his wife had shared their servant with each other. Her body was softer than Svetlana's, with larger breasts. Though not as firm as they were before, she had still aged gracefully enough for Valens to find her desirable. Svetlana guided Erin on top of Valens, who groaned loudly as he entered her. Svetlana then kissed her way down Erin's quivering body and then crawled around to where she was straddling Valens' face. The familiar pleasure that he had not experienced in over a year seemed to wash away the blight of the previous evening as the three of them were consumed in mutual ecstasy.

○

Valens had no idea how long he slept. He woke to find he was lying on his stomach, his wife gently caressing his back; Erin had left and went back to her duties. Svetlana's sweet smile contrasted with the purple bruise that had formed on her temple. She laughed when she saw him staring at it.

"People are going to look at us and think we are completely insane," he observed with a sigh as he rolled onto his side. Svetlana shrugged and started to caress his chest.

"Perhaps we are," she replied. "You know my family's people have always been a little more…*aggressive*."

"That's putting it mildly," Valens laughed. "I remember watching your brother and grandfather beat each other into oblivion on almost a daily basis." Svetlana laughed at the memory.

"Yes, Grandfather always used to say that Magnus had gone soft on him," she replied. "As strange as this may sound, he was always the most violent towards Magnus because I think he loved him the most. It was my father and Oleg who he really felt had gone soft on him, though he never said this openly. Hansi he respected well enough, but he was always very proud to see how Magnus excelled as a soldier."

"I was always grateful that he never showed this kind of 'love' towards me," Valens remarked.

"Well he probably would have, except he figured I was more than enough for you." Svetlana winked as she said this then gave him an affectionate slap on the bottom. She then leaned over and kissed him gently and started to get out of bed. "We have the Emperor's banquet tonight, so we'd best clean up."

Valens dropped his head into the pillow. He had completely forgotten about the banquet! As if on cue, Erin entered the room.

"My lady's bath is ready," she said with a bow.

"You can wash after I'm done," Svetlana said to her husband. "Women need more time to make ourselves presentable."

Chapter IV: Shadows of Intrigue

Claudia Antonia, eldest daughter of Emperor Claudius

"Rough night?" Praxus asked as Valens and Svetlana entered the great hall. Though both formally dressed, their faces still bore the marks of their violent lovemaking from earlier.

"That, and a rough morning," Valens replied with a grin. The four Master Centurions from the legions that had conquered Britannia had been given seats at the head table by the Emperor himself. While all the other guests had donned formal togas, Claudius had directed that the legions' commanding generals, Chief Tribunes, and Centurions holding the rank of Primus Ordo and above all wear ceremonial armour. This consisted of an ornate breastplate over a decorated leather cuirass. Valens could not deny that it looked impressive on Praxus, who was leading his wife, Alane, towards their seats.

For Valens this was the first time he had worn a formal toga; it had taken him twice as long as his wife to get dressed, as every fold had to placed exactly right, especially in places where it now bore the narrow purple stripe of the equites. While it stood out against the wider purple stripe that denoted senatorial patricians, it still signified that Valens was now part of the nobility. Even the lesser nobility of the equites still held large sway within the Empire. Between those born into the class, plus retired Centurions elevated to this noble order, their numbers were perhaps several thousand; several thousand out of a population that exceeded seventy million.

Earlier in the evening, whilst Erin helped him get dressed, he had expressed to his wife that he felt like a fraud.

"Don't be silly," Svetlana chastised. "You've done more to earn your place among the equites than any of those pompous senators ever did to become patricians!"

"Yes, but what does it mean to *be* a noble?" Valens had asked. "I honestly have no idea how I'm supposed to act, what protocols change now that I'm supposedly more than just a dirty soldier from the dregs of society."

"You find it ironic?" Svetlana asked, noting the perpetual grin on her husband's face.

"I find it *hilarious*," he replied with a wicked laugh.

The Senatorial Legates who had commanded the legions were already lounging on their couches. Flavius Vespasian, who had commanded the Second Legion during the invasion, had just recently returned in time for the Triumph. His brother, Flavius Sabinus, had commanded Valens' own legion, the Twentieth. Both the Emperor as well as Aulus Plautius, who had been overall commander of the invasion force, credited the two brothers with almost singlehandedly winning the war. Indeed, both Sabinus and Vespasian had proven to be highly skilled tacticians whose personal valour had made them the perfect example to their men. Vespasian had gone as far as to place himself on an impromptu ramming crew that was desperately trying to breach the gates of an enemy stronghold. That their commanding general would place himself in such a precarious position had rallied his men to renew the assault and emerge victorious.

Among the shouts of victory following that particular battle, some of the men had half-jokingly said that Vespasian was an Emperor in the making. Such remarks, harmless as they may have been, drew quick rebukes from senior officers, not least of from Vespasian himself. The last thing he needed was unfounded rumours of treason during his greatest hour. When Claudius had heard of the incident, he took it with good humour and assured the young Legate that his loyalty and valour were above reproach.

Plautius had gone as far as to suggest that the pending Triumph should be awarded to the brothers, yet Roman law forbade anyone except members of the imperial family from accepting a Triumph. A lesser Ovation parade would be conducted specifically for Sabinus and Vespasian, though many took this as an insult rather than an honour. Even the Emperor Claudius felt awkward about accepting a Triumph when he personally only spent sixteen total days in Britannia. The laws regarding Triumphs dated back to the reign of Augustus and many, including the Emperor, felt they were archaic and in need of revision. It was too late for Sabinus and Vespasian, though Claudius promised to rectify the issue for future campaigns. As a sign of his good faith, when the Senate awarded him the title of *Britannicus*, he refused to accept it for himself. Instead, he passed the name on to his son, which was an ancient tradition going back at least two hundred years to the Punic Wars.

Valens and Svetlana found their places next to some of the other Centurions. A total of eighty of Valens' peers had been selected to come to Rome for the Triumph. Their numbers, combined with their wives, as well as the large contingent of Senators, Tribunes, and other nobles, made the gigantic hall feel rather crowded. Valens figured there were several hundred guests in attendance. Praetorian Guardsmen were dispersed along the walls and he kept his eyes open to see if Cornelius was amongst them. He did not see the Praetorian Centurion and was baffled as to what he had been doing at a filthy whorehouse in the middle of the night; in uniform no less! From what he remembered, Cornelius had simply been there as an observer and was not a participant in the night's debauchery. His thoughts were interrupted when the porter at the far end of the hall slammed his staff into the floor three times; each resonating with a loud echo that immediately silenced the assembled host.

"Rise for his highness, Tiberius Claudius Drusus Caesar; Emperor of Rome and conqueror of Britannia!" All stood and gave a loud ovation as Claudius walked into the hall, his arm intertwined with that of his wife, the Empress Messalina.

Claudius was in his fifties, though he appeared older; ill health having cursed him much of his life. He did his best to walk straight, yet a clubfoot had always made him limp. His head twitched involuntarily and he was prone to stuttering. In appearance, he looked nothing like one would think the ruler of the known world should. His brother had been the legendary general, Germanicus Caesar. It was Germanicus who had destroyed the Germanic alliance and been awarded the last Triumph almost three decades before.

Though Claudius did not have his late brother's physical gifts or military prowess, his mind was what made him strong. His economic policies were sound and the people were reaping the benefits of his rule since he became Caesar three years earlier. This made him hugely popular with the masses, who for once were able to forsake the vanities of physical appearance that Roman society was quick to judge one by.

"Ave Caesar!" everyone in the hall shouted. Claudius smiled and waved for everyone to take their seats. As servants walked from table to table, offering the first round of delicacies, the entertainment began.

"From North Africa, music and dancing!" the porter shouted. A host of practically naked black women danced their way into the hall as men started to beat on a series of drums, whose rapid beat the women gyrated their bodies to. The Roman nobility was fascinated by anything considered 'foreign' to them. It was both perverse and exotic to them to watch the African women in what appeared to almost be a violent trance. Having spent part of his youth in Africa, Valens was not nearly as enraptured as the rest of the guests. A number of legionaries who his father had served with were black Africans, as were a handful that had been with Valens in Judea. If anything, it just reinforced how vast and diverse the Empire really was. The drums continued to beat, the rhythm increasing as the women matched it with their violent, yet hypnotic dancing.

They went on like this for some time; the Romans rapt in fascination at the spectacle while their senses were assailed by the rapid banging of drums. Then as suddenly as it began, the music suddenly stopped as all the women erupted into a loud shriek and then all fell to their knees before the Emperor, who started clapping enthusiastically. Not sure what else to do, the host of guests followed suit.

It was during a lull as the African dancers and drummers made their way out of the hall and the next group of entertainers made ready that Valens first caught a good look at the Empress Messalina. Though she sat on the far side of the hall from him, there was no mistaking that face. Valens' eyes grew wide, he spit out his wine as his jaw dropped and he began to sweat.

"What is it, love?" Svetlana asked.

"It's her," he breathed.

"Who?" his wife asked, scanning the room.

"Her!" He nodded his head towards the head table.

"The Empress?" Svetlana asked. "What of her?"

"Either she has a twin, or else it's *her*."

"Her *who*?" Svetlana then stared at him in disbelief. "Are you telling me the woman you violated without me was Empress Messalina? You've gone off your head!"

"I admit I was drunk out of my mind," Valens replied, "but there is no mistaking her. It all makes sense now! Cornelius was there last night, in uniform! He and another Praetorian were there as her bodyguards. I was so out of it that I didn't put it all together until just now." As he spoke, Messalina met his gaze and smiled wickedly. Keeping her eyes locked on him, she casually picked up a fig, ran it over her lips, flicked it with her tongue, and then bit down hard on it. Svetlana watched and her eyes grew wide in realization.

"Wait, did she just make a seductive gesture towards you?" She then started laughing and playfully smacked her husband on the shoulder. "I don't believe it. You *did* fuck the Empress! I have to say, I'm impressed! If only I had been there…"

"From Dacia, the acrobats of Siret!" The porter's voice and the striking of instruments as a score of acrobats tumbled onto the open floor interrupted their eye contact with the Empress.

"Excuse me, I have to step out for a moment," Valens said, rising quickly and making his way past the crowded tables for the nearest exit. However amusing Svetlana may have found his exploits with the Empress, he understood he had plunged into dangerous waters and he needed time to think. He found an empty foyer by one of the exits and his heart almost stopped when he saw a woman walking casually towards him; her face in the shadows.

"Not leaving us are you, Centurion Valens?"

"No, my lady," Valens replied, bowing low. As Messalina walked into the soft glow of the lamp light, her expression was one of almost childlike innocence; a far cry from the deviant savagery of the night before. He then gave her a quizzical look.

"How…how do you know my name?" he asked.

"Well your *rank* I know, because you told me," she replied. "As for your name, not only did I overhear it from Cornelius…" She then reached into her stola and produced a ring. Valens' eyes grew wide and his heart sank. So he had been robbed after all! It was a gold ring, given to him by his father, and his father before him. The engraved family name was still legible, even after all these years. It was really the only material thing that his family had to pass on, and it meant everything to him. He had completely forgotten that he'd kept it in his money pouch.

"I thank you for returning my ring to me," he said as he started to reach for it. The Empress slapped his hand away.

"Oh no, I think I shall keep this," she replied, holding the ring up to the light and then looking him in the eye. "It shall serve as a reminder that I own you now." Her face was still casting a look of innocence, though now her eyes betrayed a wicked blackness within. She then walked towards him until her face was but inches from his. Valens clenched his fists and tried to control his anger.

"What do you want of me?" he said through gritted teeth. She then laughed again.

"Me fein do anam," the Empress whispered into his ear. Though he had no idea what the words meant, or even what language they were, their sinister meaning caused a chill to run up his spine. Messalina then gave him a knowing smile and started to walk away. "I shall call upon you when I need your services."

Despite her physical beauty, the sight of her made his skin crawl. He felt completely emasculated and it incensed him. He did not survive more than thirty years in the legions and countless battles against those who wished to spill his guts, only to be so grievously insulted by this spoiled brat! Messalina was little more than a sullen whore. Her being Empress was only a stroke of dumb luck; she had been married off to Claudius by Caligula as a cruel joke.

Valens' rage overwhelming his senses, he started to race down the hall where she had come from. He would snap her neck and take his ring back, all else be damned! As he reached an intersection, another figure jumped out from a side passage and blocked his way.

"Stop!" It was another young woman. "Do not pursue her if you want to live!"

"Who the fuck are you to keep me from taking back what is mine?" he barked. The woman's face bore a look of surprise for a moment. She then shook her head and kept her composure.

"My name is Claudia Antonia," she replied. Valens took a step back and dropped his head, embarrassed.

"Forgive me, my lady," he said, immediately regaining his composure once he realized he had just insulted the Emperor's daughter. Messalina was gone and he had no idea now which way she went.

"Come with me," Antonia said quietly. Before he could answer, she took him by the arm and led him out of a side passage that led to a concealed garden. A young man dressed in a resplendent toga with a broad purple stripe was waiting for them, pacing nervously.

"This is my husband, Pompey Magnus," Antonia explained. "Husband, this is Centurion Valens…the latest victim of Messalina's web of deceit."

"I know who you are," Valens said with a short bow. "You are the last of a noble line."

"So they tell me," Pompey said dryly. "I feel for you, having become caught up in that wicked girl's scheming."

"What do you mean scheming?" Valens asked. "I was drunk and wandered into a brothel one night by accident! She used me as a play thing, nothing more."

"She will use you for more than that before she's done with you," Antonia replied. "And there is nothing you can do to stop her. Her whoring herself out at her own private brothel is the worst kept secret in the entire city…"

"To everyone except your father, I am guessing," Valens interrupted. Antonia nodded. She was short of stature and very young, even younger than Messalina. Despite this, her eyes showed a far greater intelligence than her stepmother, along with a knack for survival that she had inherited from her father.

"He will hear no unkind words against her, not even from me," she explained. "Anyone foolish enough to try and tell my father of her transgressions will be signing their own death sentence. She spews poison into his ear, and he thinks it is honey!"

"So where do you fit into all this?" Valens asked Pompey.

"As you said, I am the last of a great line," the young man explained. "Being married to the Emperor's daughter, I am a threat to her son."

"Your brother?" Valens asked Antonia, who rolled her eyes in reply.

"As you are well aware, Messalina has taken a lot more seed into her than just that of my father, including yours!" she scoffed. "I know not whether Britannicus and Octavia are my brother and sister. Father believes without a doubt they are his and what matters is that Messalina is determined Britannicus becomes the next Emperor of Rome."

"Well if Claudius is convinced that he is his son, that would be the logical progression of things," Valens reasoned. "I fail to see a problem."

"Britannicus is but an infant!" Pompey retorted. "Rome is not like the corrupt kingdoms of the east that place children on the thrones of power, yet Messalina is determined that her son does just that. Claudius is not a young man and he has never been in good health. Should he die before Britannicus comes of age, there will be chaos. Messalina fears that people may turn to me as a viable heir to the imperial throne, given my lineage and marriage. Despite the ignominious end of my Triumvir ancestor, my name is still one the people respect. And like you were quick to point out, I am the last of that line."

"Look," Valens replied with a sigh. "I don't mean to sound unsympathetic, but the intricacies within the imperial household are not my problem. I'm supposed to be *retiring* from public service! All I want is to collect my pension, get my ring back, take my wife, and leave Rome."

"If you are wise, you will leave Rome immediately," Pompey remarked.

"No, I cannot leave until I get back what is mine," Valens retorted.

"And yet, as long as Messalina feels she has a use for you, she will never let you leave the city," Antonia added coldly. "You're going down a dark path, Centurion Valens. As you are one who has spent his lifetime protecting the Empire's borders, I pray you will be able to escape from Messalina's clutches before it is too late."

Valens returned the banquet and sat brooding in silence for the rest of the night. Svetlana had drunk to excess and he had to help her to a waiting litter that would take them home. All the while he held a deep suspicion that they were being watched. He could feel several sets of eyes on him as he carried his giggling wife through the gate of the house.

Chapter V: The Last Triumph

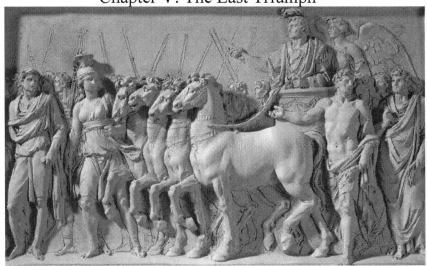

A Roman Triumph, from the *Arch of Titus*, Rome

The arrival of the day of the Triumphal parade was a welcome reprieve to Valens. For days, he brooded over the implausible events that had somehow drawn him into the web of the Empress Messalina. Had he never gone to the imperial banquet, he would have eventually dismissed the night in the brothel as a dream brought on by extreme drunkenness, and would have lamented the disappearance of his family ring as negligible loss. However, no wine or other mind-altering substances passed his lips the night of the banquet. The reality of his transgressions and their as yet unknown consequences haunted him.

After decades of battling Rome's fiercest enemies, how had he let himself be bested by a sullen whore like Messalina? The question vexed him greatly. It had been deceit that had been his undoing, not physical or mental prowess. Supposing he did take Pompey Magnus' advice and simply left Rome? That was fine, but then there would always been the fear of what would happen should Messalina decide to make an example of him, show the ring bearing his name to Claudius, and concoct some story about how she got it. No, to run away would not only fail to solve the problem, it was simply not in Valens' nature to be a coward. By the time he had to report to the local barracks and get accountability of his men, Valens had further reasoned that perhaps this was not such a dire situation after all. If the Empress was in such need of his services, then perhaps he could wield this situation to his advantage.

The parade itself would stretch for miles. The Emperor would ride in his private chariot, accompanied by his children. As was custom, a slave stood behind him with a laurel crown held over his head. During the parade, he would whisper to Claudius, "Remember, you are just a man." This unusual tradition dated back to the Republic, where triumphant generals during their highest moment of glory would be reminded by the humblest that like them, they were but mortal men. Spoils taken from the province, along with chained prisoners of war, would be displayed to the populace. The legionaries who had conquered the province would be the last to march through Rome.

Valens checked himself over, making certain that the harness bearing his awards and campaign medals fit properly over his armour. Erin had taken the time to polish the embossed discs, as well as his helmet. He marvelled that today would be the last day he would wear his armour and draw his sword for Rome. For the time being, his ongoing perverse saga with the Empress Messalina did not matter.

"It will be about another hour before we begin," Centurion Praxus said as he walked over to where Valens and his men were gathered.

"I wouldn't expect anything this large to start on time," the Centurion grunted. His expression was vacant and his friend picked up on it.

"Valens are you alright?" Praxus asked. "You've been acting funny ever since we got to Rome."

"To be honest, I'm not real sure," Valens replied. "I'll explain another time."

"Fair enough," the Centurion Primus Ordo replied. "Hard to believe it's been almost three decades since we last did one of these."

"Feels like it was in another lifetime," Valens replied. Praxus was one of the few faces that he recognized from that era.

"Soldiers in the ranks have come and gone," Praxus agreed. "You realize that some of the lads who had joined after the Triumph of Germanicus Caesar completed their entire terms of service and were discharged long before we invaded Britannia."

"Don't say things like that, it makes me feel old," Valens retorted with a short laugh. His face was then sombre. "And others left the ranks on pyres of fire and ash, having fallen in what the ignorant masses call *glorious service to the Empire*." Praxus snorted in reply.

"There are many who will never understand," he concurred. "There is honour in fighting for one's nation; there might even be a trace of nobility in what we do. But glory? No! There is no glory in this. Over the years, all our friends who we burned on funeral pyres, was there any glory in how they died? I don't care how elaborate of a spectacle we put on this day, it is all a façade."

"Twentieth Legion...fall in!" the shouted order came from the Master Centurion.

"Let's go and fool the masses one last time," Valens said with a smile as he donned his helmet and walked briskly over to his men.

The cheers of the adoring crowds were deafening. Valens knew not where his wife and her family would be in the massed throng that numbered in the tens-of-thousands. For a brief moment, he was allowed to reflect back on his career in the legions that had taken up his entire adult life. He had served with great men, fought in some of Rome's fiercest battles, and been part of the very bonds that held the Empire together. Whether the Senate and nobility recognized it or not, the common people knew that it was the armoured legionaries who held the beacon of Rome's light, who protected them in the night from unspeakable horrors, and who brought that light to the darkest corners of the world. *That* was the nobility which Praxus had spoken of and that knowledge made Valens realize that the last thirty years of his life had not been spent in vain. The cold reality was that the world was an ugly and dark place. Soldiers like Valens sacrificed enormously, often their very lives, to keep that light of civilization going. And so, as the Triumphal parade passed it was the formations of soldiers who received the loudest accolades; louder than even the cheers for the Emperor. Valens took it all in allowed himself to enjoy the adulation of the mob.

Since there was only a partial representation from each legion, Valens had none of his senior officers with him. Only twenty men had been allowed to come from each century, and of these there were but two decani, the sergeants of legionaries. One of these men carried the century's standard as he marched next to his centurion. Valens kept his eyes on the Legion's eagle standard, which was carried at the front of the formation, next to the master centurion. When he saw the standard tilted forward, he knew they were close to the reviewing stand.

"Gladius…draw!" he called over his shoulder.

"Rah!" his men shouted as they unsheathed their swords. Both consuls, as well as the more prominent senators, stood under an ornate canopy that shielded them from the glaring sun. The highly polished armour and swords of the legionaries shone brightly, blinding them with the glare. As Valens raised his weapon in salute, he almost fell out of step when he saw the Empress Messalina, along with her mother, at the centre of the reviewing stand.

"Sir, I think the Empress just waved at you," the Decanus carrying the Signum said to him.

"Well then, she knows excellence when she sees it," he replied cynically. The Decanus had been speaking in jest, yet he was more right than he knew. For Valens, there was no mistaking Messalina's gesture towards him. In spite of his being but one among many, with his face partially covered by his helmet, she still noticed him. It was almost as if she was watching for him. From a distance, he could not tell if her smile bore a good omen or ill.

Chapter VI: Web of Deceit

Praetorian Guardsmen

The loud banging on the front door startled Valens as he sat to breakfast. He sensed right away who was waiting on the other side before slaves opened the door. Svetlana reached over and clutched his hand as Cornelius and a handful of Praetorian Guardsmen entered the dining hall.

"Your presence is required by the Emperor," Cornelius said. There was no threat in his tone and Valens could only speculate as to why Claudius would wish to see him. He was but one officer amongst many in Rome for the Triumph, so he suspected that it had to have something to do with Messalina; there could be no other explanation. The realization made his blood run cold. He embraced his wife hard and started towards the door. The Praetorian Centurion's next words made his blood run cold.

"Your presence is required as well," Cornelius said to Svetlana. Valens started to protest, but knew there was nothing he could do. He clutched his wife's hand as they made the long trek in silence to the imperial palace. Two squads of Praetorians flanked them, with Cornelius taking the lead.

It therefore surprised Valens when he entered the administrative offices of the Emperor and saw Centurion Praxus, along with several other officers. All were talking jovially amongst themselves.

"Praxus, what the hell are we doing here?" Valens asked. His friend simply smiled and shrugged.

"I have no idea," he replied. "But this is the first time in my life that I've had the chance to meet an Emperor, and I'm not going to waste it."

Valens then noticed that Alane, along with the wives of the other officers were also present. Svetlana, who was still oblivious to her husband's vexation, walked over to Alane and embraced her affectionately. The two started bantering immediately. Valens let out a deep sigh of relief; for all he knew, the Emperor was oblivious to his transgressions with Messalina. At length, a group of freedmen clerks and a pair of Tribunes entered from the far doorway. One turned and addressed the group.

"His imperial highness, Tiberius Claudius Drusus Caesar!" the man boomed. All bowed as the Emperor limped into the room, Messalina guiding him by the arm. Her appearance made Valens uneasy, though she pretended not to notice him.

"My friends!" Claudius said with enthusiasm, a broad smile adorning his face.

In truth, Valens could not help but be taken by the Emperor. Claudius' physical infirmities would have meant his death in other societies. Even Rome had a history of leaving infants of less than acceptable physical attributes exposed to die. Thankfully for Claudius, the Emperor Augustus had abolished such horrid practices.

Throughout Claudius' life, the imperial family had gone through many periods of upheaval as its members subtly fought against each other in a fatal struggle to attain ultimate power. Playing up his afflictions, exaggerating his stutter, and acting like an incompetent fool, he had kept such a low profile that he was often not noticed. Oddly enough, his predecessor and nephew, Gaius Caligula, had been rather fond of him. Caligula would occasionally play what he felt were humorous jokes on him; the irony being one of those was his current marriage. Three years before Caligula's death, he thought it would be the ultimate punch line to marry his forty-eight year old uncle off to the beautiful Messalina, who was only seventeen at the time. Valens reasoned that given the web of deceit she used to blind Claudius, Caligula did get the last laugh after all.

"A...all of you are here today because you are at the end of your g...glorious careers," the Emperor continued. "Your triumph over the Britons is a fitting monument to your m...many personal achievements. It is an honour for me to personally present you all with y...your discharge papers and pensions from the army." He then turned to the Tribunes and nodded. One held a stack of scrolls, which he would hand to the Emperor as the other read names off the list.

"Centurion Primus Ordo Gaius Praxus!" Valens beamed as he watched his old friend, whose career he had been a part of his own, step forward and face the Emperor. Out of the corner of his eye, Valens could see Alane wiping a tear from her eye, her face showing the deep sense of pride in her husband. Claudius and Praxus exchanged a few quiet words as the Emperor handed him the scroll bearing his discharge orders. They clasped hands and Praxus saluted before turning and walking back to the group. The names of the other men were called, and each came forward to receive his retirement orders from the Emperor. It was indeed a deep honour; one that but a few would ever receive. For some reason, Valens was not surprised that he was the last to be called forward. Granted this could have been for no other reason than he was the most junior ranking officer amongst the assembly; all the rest of the men had been Cohort Commanders or senior.

"Centurion Tiberius Valens!" Valens had to stifle a chuckle as he heard a quick squeal of delight from Svetlana. His troubles momentarily forgotten, he stepped forward and stood face to face with the Emperor, who took the last remaining scroll from the Tribune. The expression on Claudius' face reassured him that this was the first time the Emperor had heard mention of his name.

"Y...you've had quite the distinguished career," Claudius said. "Rome is f...forever in your debt."

"Thank you, Caesar," Valens replied, taking the scroll and then clasping the Emperor's hand. He quickly saluted and returned to where Svetlana stood waiting for him. She placed her arm around his shoulders and kissed him on the cheek.

"These clerks will take you to the holding area where your pensions await you," one of the Tribunes said as the group started to mingle once more. "Armed escorts are available, at your discretion, to take you as far as the city's boundaries." This was a much-appreciated practicality in the minds of the now-retired soldiers. After all, since all of them were Centurions or higher, their pensions were substantial; which made a perfect target for robbers. Valens started to follow the crowd out of the room when his way was blocked by both the Emperor and Empress.

"Centurion V...Valens," Claudius said. "My wife has met with the other men and their wives, but had not had a chance to meet you. She insisted that she have the ch...chance to do so before you leave us."

"Highness," Valens said, bowing his head.

"Please, the honour is mine," Messalina said sweetly. "And this must be your wife..."

"Svetlana," Svetlana said as the Empress took both of her hands in hers.

"A name of the north," Messalina observed. "The beauty and strength of your people is unmatched." Svetlana blushed and smiled. It baffled Valens that his wife was enjoying herself. Then again, she did not comprehend the danger that Messalina presented.

"Husband," Messalina said, turning to address Claudius, "I would like to borrow a few minutes of Centurion Valens' time before he leaves us."

"I c...can deny you nothing, my love," Claudius replied. Valens felt his skin crawl as the Empress took him by the arm and led him to an outside balcony that overlooked an ornate garden. He could hear the Emperor exchanging pleasantries with Svetlana as he and Messalina continued to walk. His wife was speaking very quickly, excited as she was to have her own audience with the Emperor.

"Your wife is very lovely," Messalina said once they were out of earshot.

"What do you want?" Valens asked impatiently.

"Do not even think about getting impertinent with me," the Empress retorted. Though her expression remained unchanged, her voice had turned to ice. "Remember, I *own* you, even if Rome does not anymore. You will learn that soon enough. You will also learn that I always get what I want, and I want your wife."

"What are you going to do with her?" Valens asked; his heart in his throat. Messalina shrugged nonchalantly.

"Only what I do with all women who catch my fancy," she replied. "There are certain erogenous areas that a woman is more capable of tending to than a man. Your wife knows this. I could see the curious lust in her eyes. You will bring her to me tonight. I will have you escorted, lest you lose your way."

"I'm sure we'll manage," Valens remarked.

"Don't take me for a fool," Messalina said as she dug her fingernails into his arm. "I'll have Cornelius escort you home. You two are old acquaintances and I think it best that you spend some time catching up before you bring the lovely Svetlana to me."

It was a long trek back to Ostia. Cornelius had arranged for a pair of litters and had insisted on riding with Valens.

"You should leave now while you can," the Praetorian said as they were carried through the raucous streets of Rome by more than a dozen slaves. The litter they rode in was completely enclosed, ensuring the privacy of their conversation.

"Not while that bitch has my family ring!" Valens retorted angrily.

"Fuck your ring!" Cornelius snapped. "It is but a trinket..." Valens' attempt to lunge at the Praetorian almost tipped the litter over. Outside the slaves were chastised loudly by the Guardsmen who walked beside them.

"How dare you mock the loss to my family's honour!" he barked, as he fell back to his seat. For the first time, Cornelius showed emotion as his face grew red and his eyes clouded with rage.

"You want to speak of honour?" he growled in a low voice. "You have no idea the blight on my honour, or the loss I have suffered." Valens cooled his temper, realizing he had tread dangerously with Cornelius. "My wife..."

"Rebekkah," Valens replied. "I remember her; she was a Judean that you met in Caesarea. Absolutely lovely woman."

"She's dead," Cornelius said coldly.

"I am sorry," Valens replied; lowering his head as his friend's eyes bore into him.

"She is dead because of that bitch I am forced to serve," Cornelius continued. "As you have gathered, Messalina likes to use both men and women for sport."

"Did she ever use you?" The question caught the Praetorian off guard, but he nodded and continued.

"I suppose I should start at the beginning; at least from the time of the Emperor's accession. You should know that *I* was one of the Praetorians who made Claudius Emperor. Once Gaius Caligula was slain, we had to find ourselves a successor quickly, lest the Empire fall into chaos. Many of us who served in the far reaches of the Empire knew that Rome had become far too big to be effectively ruled as a Republic; though for the pompous fools who had become Praetorians by political connection, they needed an Emperor lest they get sent to the legions. Me and two squads found Caligula's uncle hiding behind a curtain. Since it had been our deputy prefect, Cassius Chaerea, who had killed Caligula, Claudius thought for certain that we would murder him too."

"I never did condone what Claudius did to Cassius," Valens remarked. "Murdering Caligula saved us from a tyrannical despot who fancied himself a living god. To say nothing of the fact that Caligula's death led to Claudius' ascension."

"You must remember," Cornelius conjectured, "that Claudius never wanted to be Emperor. It is a burden he took reluctantly, not too differently than his uncle Tiberius a generation before. He regarded Cassius as a hero of the Empire for what he did in Teutoburger Wald all those years ago, when he saved the lives of more than a hundred legionaries. Unfortunately, Cassius' rage towards Caligula had spread to utter hatred for the entire imperial family. The conspirators had agreed that only Caligula should die; something that Claudius felt he could not with a clear conscious condemn them for, as he spared the others. But Cassius had taken it upon himself to also murder Caligula's wife and young daughter. He was actively hunting down Claudius and his family, but thankfully my lads found him first. The Emperor had no choice but to condemn Cassius, though it pained all of us who had to carry out his sentence."

"Still, Claudius had to have been personally very grateful to you," Valens observed. Cornelius nodded.

"Yes," he replied. "Which brings us to the Empress Messalina. Claudius was indeed grateful to me, and to my men. I have a vote of confidence with him that few enjoy. The only person who he trusts more is the Empress. Even I cannot let him know of her adulteries without condemning myself. In a bit of twisted irony, Claudius assigned me as Messalina's personal guard, as a type of reward for my service." He paused for a minute and gazed at the floor of the litter. Outside they could hear the clamour of the busy metropolis growing softer and Valens knew they were almost to the city gates. After a few minutes of silence, Cornelius looked up at him once more.

"It was almost immediately after taking my assignment that I was exposed to her treachery and evil. She offered me wine one night when it was just the two of us in her study. The Emperor was off on an inspection of the harbours in Neapolis and was expected to be gone a week or more. Messalina had expressed her desire to accompany him, only she had come down with one of her headaches; or so she told him. Seems she gets 'headaches' quite often and only travels with the Emperor just enough to keep his suspicions in check. For all he knows, she is the utterly faithful and devoted wife."

"Yes, I heard mutterings about the questionable paternity of their two children," Valens added.

"I think there's as good a chance they are mine as his," Cornelius replied with dark humour. He then continued, "That night, she offered me wine that had been laced with opiate. I laid with her, much to my later shame and disgust. I learned to check my emotions, as if I ever showed any signs of revulsion or awkwardness, it would only entice her to take me into her bed. She later became intrigued with Rebekkah, calling her an exotic woman that she had to have for herself. I protested, but the Empress is not one who accepts rejection. The more I resisted, the more determined she became to have my wife as her plaything. Without my knowledge, she invited Rebekkah to a private banquet she was having. When I saw them together it was already too late. Messalina had drugged my wife and was taking her to the back room of the brothel. Her expression dared me to try and stop her. When she came out of her drug-induced state, my wife completely broke. You remember that she was a Judean. She was also a follower of the prophet they called 'Christ', who we had executed years ago. As such, her guilt at the thought of betraying me by fornicating with another woman was unbearable. She would not look at me, nor talk to me except to break down in sorrow, pleading with me for forgiveness. I could not console her or take her in my arms without her breaking.

"I don't know what happened in that room, though in the darkest corners of my mind I can only guess. Rebekkah killed herself not long after. After insisting that she help me out of my kit one evening, she took my sword and slashed her own throat." Cornelius paused again as the words sank in to Valens. He tried to understand that Rebekkah had been of a culture that was completely foreign to both him and Svetlana. Though he would not say it aloud, Valens suspected that Cornelius' wife had been violated by more than just the Empress Messalina. He pitied his friend for the twisted torment of having to protect the very woman who had taken his wife from him.

"If you have nothing left to live for, why don't you just kill Messalina and be done with it?" Cornelius' face hardened at the question.

"You think I don't want to? Every day I have to stay my hand from striking down that wicked cunt. You forget I have two sons and a daughter, who I love more than life itself. If I murder the Empress, what happens to them?"

"I understand," Valens sympathized. "Have you ever considered remarrying?" It was an awkward question on the surface, though a logical one.

"I have," Cornelius replied. "There is a woman; the daughter of a Plebeian Tribune, that I've grown rather fond of. However, I dare not remarry while the Empress Messalina lives. Understand this, Valens, I *will* kill Messalina! She is not very intelligent, and sooner or later she will make a fatal error. She fancies herself as being the Empress Livia reborn! Livia was shrewd and possessed a vast intellect. She found ways of ruling through Augustus, yet she was also completely devoted to him and to the Empire. Messalina is only devoted to the next hit of opiate, and the next victim that she chooses to spread her legs for. I swear before God and all that I love, that not only will I kill Messalina, it will be the Emperor himself who orders me to do it!"

Chapter VII: Empress of Lust

Messalina working in a brothel, by Agostino Carracci (late 16th century etching)

Though Valens felt trapped in Messalina's web, Svetlana was rather giddy with excitement as they entered the Empress' private brothel. Unlike the last time he was there, it was mostly empty. A handful of courtesans, along with a squad of Praetorians, serving as bodyguards, were the only people there. They were escorted to a different room that Valens did not remember seeing before. It was quite large, with lamps and incense burners hanging from the ceiling, leaving a pungent aroma in the air.

The Empress was adorned in a sheer gown that revealed her body through the lamp light. She handed Svetlana a chalice of wine, though Valens wondered if that was all it contained.

"You are most welcome, my dear," Messalina said sweetly as she caressed the Norsewoman's cheek.

"Thank you, my lady," Svetlana replied with a smile. She was taller than the Empress, who appeared to be enraptured by her strength. Valens took a long pull off what he knew to be laced wine, longing for the intoxication that would make him for a moment forget that he was in a wicked place. Under most circumstances this would not have bothered him, but the longer he spent in the clutches of the Empress, the more sinister his feelings became. She wanted him for something, and it was not just sexual gratification. Such realizations ruined whatever sense of erotic adventure he would have normally felt.

Messalina placed both hands on Svetlana's cheeks and started to kiss her tenderly on the lips. Valens' mind started to cloud and he allowed himself a smile. It was hard to believe that the beautiful young woman who was now kissing his wife with added passion was at the root of so much evil. She was so young; young enough to be his daughter in fact. In public, her demeanour was one of piety and innocence, along with absolute devotion to her husband, the Emperor. That Claudius had completely fallen for the façade was in complete contrast to the level-headed pragmatism which he ruled the Roman Empire with.

Well, what concern is it of mine if he's too dim-witted to see through her web of deceit? he thought quietly to himself as his mind pleasantly clouded.

Messalina had guided Svetlana to the oversized bed and laid her down. It gave her a feeling of power to be able to control the striking Nordic woman who was inherently far stronger than she. Svetlana was completely naked and lying on her back, face glowing in ecstasy. Messalina had removed her garments as well and was kneeling over her lover, kissing her breasts and running her tongue over each in turn. As she kneeled over his wife with her cute butt in the air, Valens could not help but appreciate how firm her body was, even after having born two children in recent years.

Whereas Messalina had been demanding that Valens do everything to service her, she was instead doing all the work as Svetlana laid back with her arms stretched over her head, groaning in pleasure. Messalina kissed her way down her torso and buried her face between Svetlana's legs. With her skilled tongue, she caused the Nordic woman to scream once more in ecstasy as she was sent over the edge. It was the last thing Valens saw as his vision faded.

Valens was startled awake as a bucket of water was splashed on him. He bolted upright and immediately fell back down, his head throbbing.

"Where the hell am I?" he asked groggily.

"Some special quarters I had arranged for you," he heard Messalina say from the shadowed doorway. "You and your lovely wife had a bit too much to drink last night and so I kept you here as my guests."

"That was no ordinary wine," Valens observed as he rolled onto his side and felt Svetlana lying next to him, still passed out from the drugged vintage they had consumed.

"I couldn't very well have you wandering the streets in the middle of the night, now could I?" Messalina replied as she stepped into the soft lamp light. Valens had started to grow accustomed to the wicked grin that creased her face any time her husband was not around.

"What do you want?" Valens asked. "If you needed to keep us around as your playthings, you only had to ask." The Empress burst into laughter at his remark.

"So full of vanity, you are!" she spat. "I've had my fill of old Centurions and their Nordic wives for the time being. Did you really think I was only keeping you for sexual gratification? No, I have a *special* task for you." It was then that Valens began to sense the full danger of what Cornelius had eluded to.

"I am at your service," he replied with a nervous shrug.

"Good," the Empress replied. "For this task will not be quite as enjoyable as the last one. I have need of your *other* skills."

"Other skills?"

"Yes," Messalina said, her eyes growing dark. "You're still skilled with a blade, are you not?"

"I'm retired from that," Valens emphasized quickly. "I fought in battles against Rome's enemies; I am not a murderer!" With a sly grin, Messalina produced his ring from her stola.

"I wonder what my husband would say if he ever saw this," she said casually. "I would hate for him to hear that you tried to take advantage of me, and in a panic dropped it as you fled."

"You vile bitch!" Valens growled through gritted teeth. Messalina only laughed at his audacity to insult her. Her expression then became serious once more.

"Work for me, Valens," she said in a tone that was suddenly civil. The Centurion could not tell if it was a request or not. "We are not so different, you and I." As much as he hated to admit it, it was true. Valens was certainly no example of moral piety. He had taken more women into his bed over the years than he could count. He had spread his seed from one corner of the Empire to the other. Though he had no children that he knew of, he suspected that there were probably a number of bastards from Britannia to Judea who bore a resemblance to him.

"There is much we could do for each other," Messalina continued, "so let us not be enemies." Her voice was sweet once more; a complete contrast to the viper's tongue that had assailed him moments before.

"What do you need my sword for?" he asked. "You have a detachment of Praetorians at your disposal."

"Praetorians are not expendable," Messalina replied. She caught the twitch on Valens' face and quickly explained, "not that I think you are expendable, my love. But you must realize that the Praetorian Guard is a very public organization. Their faces are well known within the city. What should happen if one of them were spotted performing a…*service* for me? Rumour would spread that Claudius was resorting to underhanded methods for dealing with his enemies, rather than doing so openly. Imagine if a Guardsman were to have to explain his actions to the Emperor? The Praetorians know the great risk involved, and that is why this is the one task I cannot compel them to perform. They will help arrange matters for you, but they will not be the ones to strike."

"Fair enough," Valens replied. He was still angered by the Empress, yet his own tone had softened considerably. "You said we can help each other, so what's in this for me?" Messalina grinned triumphantly and walked over to a cabinet where she removed a pouch that she tossed to him. It landed heavily in his lap.

"A down payment," she explained. "Don't worry, Centurion Valens, I pay *very* well. Perform your services thoroughly and discreetly, and you shall be rewarded appropriately. I dare say, in a year's time you could double the pension that took you thirty years in the legions." Valens cringed inside at the thought of Messalina having that many enemies she needed disposed of. Still, if the price was right, he supposed that dispatching of a few dregs from the gutter was no different than killing renegade barbarians on the frontier.

"Did you set this all up?" he asked after a minute's pause to let everything sink in. Messalina laughed once more.

"Sorry to say, but no," she replied, shaking her head. "I've needed someone with your skill for some time. There are many who need a permanent lesson in what it means to earn my displeasure." Her face darkened for a moment.

"I'm impressed that you are able to hide your wickedness both in public and from your husband." Valens' grin disarmed Messalina from rebuking him. If he was willing to whore himself out as her private assassin, then a little candor could be overlooked.

"The one difference between us," she remarked, "is that while I hide my darker side, yours is displayed plain as day." It was yet another reminder for the retired Centurion that he did not hold the moral high ground with the Empress.

"It was simply a happy coincidence that you stumbled into my lair," she continued to explain. "I knew opportunity would arise with so many legionaries in Rome for the Triumph. Yet I thought much effort would have to be put forth to find a suitable candidate. After all, I cannot have one who is expected back in the ranks, or one who might have a trace of conscience. And I certainly did not expect to have one so suitable wander right into my den; it was as if Nemesis herself had sent you to me!

"I decided to entice you first and get a feel for your suitability before I put you to use. That you are married complicated things, as it meant you had something worth living for. Still, this was but a temporary setback. Your wife is an absolute delight!" Valens found he could not help but smile at the last remark.

"She seems very fond of you."

"Yes," Messalina replied with a smile. "I rather enjoy her company, and she mine. What kind of husband would you be to deny her so? Come, let us be friends." She reached her hand out, and before he knew it, Valens took it in his own and kissed the back of it.

"I am at your service, my lady." He did not notice the sinister glint in the Empress' eye.

Chapter VIII: Empress of Death
***

Despite the warmth of the summer night and the cloak wrapped around him, Valens' blood ran cold. He knew the client's face; for Messalina had made sure he memorized it through the fog of opiate smoke in the brothel. The man was the son of a wealthy merchant who supplied the imperial palace with the Claudius' favourite stock of Spanish wines. The young man was threatening to expose Messalina's den of iniquity, and using his father to gain access to the Emperor. Though he looked scarcely old enough to require a shave, there was only one way to handle a potential blackmailer.

"You must follow him and strike when he is well away from here," the Empress had ordered Valens. "Let his death mark well the fate of any who would dare threaten me!"

His palms were sweating as he watched from behind the curtain of a private booth. The two bodyguards who had accompanied the merchant's son were being repeatedly offered drink by some of the serving girls. He had no doubt that Messalina hoped to drug them so as to make Valens' task easier.

"Get off!" one of them barked as he shoved the girl away.

"Oh come now," his friend said with a friendly elbow to the ribs. "One little drink's not going to do us in."

"You know what the master said," the first bodyguard replied warily. "Last time I got piss drunk while on shift he had me flogged and docked a month's pay!"

"But this is the Empress' own private stock," the serving girl pleaded. "It came all the way from Hispania. Surely you will not disrespect her hospitality towards you." Valens suspected that if the men knew of their master's quarrels with Messalina they would have been more steadfast in their refusal. Instead, they allowed the serving woman to pour them each a small goblet, which they greedily drank from. They quickly returned the cups to the servant's tray, lest the merchant's son finish his debaucheries early and catch them drinking.

It was not long before he appeared from behind one of the curtained rooms, grinning inanely and grabbing at his crotch. With a boisterous laugh, he slapped both bodyguards on the shoulder, grabbed his cloak, and bounded up the steps. Valens then caught site of Messalina, who appeared from behind the curtain of the back hallway. He nodded at her and followed the men out.

As was usual, the ally was devoid of activity. Only a couple of drunken vagrants lay in the gutters, babbling to themselves incoherently. The bodyguards were laughing; quietly at first, but then growing noticeably louder as they made their way through the back streets.

"Shut the fuck up already!" their master barked as he turned abruptly. He did not even notice Valens lurking in the shadows but ten feet from them. "What has gotten into you two?"

"S...sorry, master," one of the men said before erupting into a fit of laughter. The merchant's son's face grew red.

"You've been drinking on duty, when you're supposed to be protecting me!" he bellowed; his voice echoing in the night. He slapped the first bodyguard, who fell to the ground, still laughing at the top of his lungs even as his master kicked him in the stomach. As Valens started to draw his gladius, he noticed that the man had dropped his weapon into the gutter; a spiked hammer.

"And you!" the young man shouted to the other bodyguard. "I've warned you about this before!" He then proceeded to punch the man repeatedly in the chest, as the other passed out from the effects of the drink.

Valens crept over as the two men tussled and picked up the hammer. Though he would have liked to have gotten further away from the brothel, he knew he had to strike. The bodyguard stumbled and hit his head on the wall, falling face first onto the street. It was then that the master noticed the Centurion.

"Who the bloody fuck..." he started to say as Valens slammed the spike on the backside of the hammer into his neck. His eyes grew wide as blood spurted from the punctured artery. The Centurion left the weapon imbedded in the man's neck as he fell to the ground, grasping at his throat for a few short seconds before he expired.

○

Messalina was surprised to see Valens returned so quickly. She was reclined back on a couch, with Svetlana's head resting on her shoulder. The Empress ran her fingers playfully through the sleeping Norsewoman's hair, who was snoring quietly.

"It is done then?"

"Exactly as you wished," Valens replied.

"My, you *are* efficient!" Messalina mused. Valens shrugged in reply.

"When one spends three decades in my former profession, you learn to kill quickly." He could not help but smile, despite the horror of the vile task he had just completed. Whether it was at the Empress' behest or not, Valens was now a murderer. He had killed a fellow Roman in cold blood; a Roman who had neither wronged him personally, nor was an enemy of the state. The way he had left the scene, his bodyguard would most likely take the blame, leading to the death of another innocent.

Valens may have been a sexual deviant with questionable morality, but he was an honourable man at heart, and as such he was repelled by his own actions. And yet, he was now beginning to understand Cornelius' warning. He had indeed fallen into Messalina's web.

The Empress snapped her fingers and a slave woman stepped forward, carrying a small bag, which she handed to Valens. He looked inside and was shocked to see several gold pieces inside.

"This is over two hundred denarii!" he said; shocked that he was being paid almost a year's pay for a legionary for having committed a single murder.

"Yes," Messalina replied, continuing to play with Svetlana's hair. "I told you that if you worked for me you would be greatly compensated. Do you like her?" She was referring to the slave woman; a young Greek of average height, with a shapely figure. The revealing garb left her shoulders and stomach exposed. Valens could not help but be aroused.

"She is very beautiful," he observed. Messalina smiled sweetly at him.

"Feel free to take her to one of the other rooms," she replied. "Consider it a bonus for your efficiency. She's quite good, I promise; I've had her myself."

Having just committed murder for money, the thought of violating a Greek slave woman while his wife slept in the Empress' arms seemed of little consequence. Valens took the woman by the arm and led her to a back room, where a pair of slaves held open the beaded curtain for him.

The woman said not a word as she let her clothes fall to the floor, revealing a pair of smaller, yet firm breasts and shapely hips that contrasted nicely with her tiny waist. Valens quickly pulled off his tunic and took her into his arms, throwing her onto the waiting bed that was still warm and had an aroma like it had been used by another fornicating couple just recently. Perhaps his wife and the Empress had shared this very bed while he was out slamming a spike through another man's neck in a dark alley. He called for wine, wishing to rid his mind of the guilt that was creeping in.

The guilt was something he had not anticipated. He thought he could rationalize his actions, yet when he saw the young man's eyes grow wide in stark horror, he knew he had committed a grievous crime.

He threw himself onto the woman and started running his tongue over her breasts and down her stomach as another slave came in with a tray bearing a wine pitcher. Valens greedily drank, knowing that it was laced with the Empress' special opiate. He then looked at the woman bearing the tray, and with a wicked grin he grabbed her by the stola and pulled her onto the bed with them. The wine pitcher spilled its remaining contents onto the three of them, as well as the bed. Valens thought it fitting that the sticky sweet liquid should mix with the sweat and other bodily fluids that merged into a pungent concoction of wicked ecstasy.

Chapter IX: A Thief's Punishment
***

A week had passed since Valens had killed the merchant's son and not a word had been spoken by anyone. It was as if the whole episode had never occurred. The leather pouch with the gold coins was the only evidence which proved that Valens had committed murder. He turned one gold aureus over in his fingers. It was an older coin; from the time of Augustus. The long dead Emperor's face seemed to scold him. Valens quickly stuffed the coin back in its pouch.

    He decided to take a walk along the Appian Way in order to clear his mind. The air was warm and pleasant, with a gentle breeze blowing through his hair. He walked in the grass beside the main road, taking in the sites and the quiet that existed outside the city. He recognized a dirt road that ran to the north, which led to the family home of his old friend, Artorius. It was then that he realized he'd been walking for several hours and he was hungry. He walked over to a grove of fruit trees and picked himself a couple of apples. As he strolled back towards the road, a pair of cloaked figures on horseback approached him. He casually walked towards the men, keeping his free hand on the pommel of his gladius, which he kept concealed beneath his own cloak. Once he got close enough, Valens noted that each man wore a gold ring on his right hand. It was then he knew who the men were and he hazarded a guess as to what they wanted.

    "Lost, are we?" Valens asked sarcastically. "Or is the Emperor out for a stroll as well?" The cloaked Praetorians glared at him.

    "We bring a message for you, *sir*," one of them said. An underlying resentment had existed for generations between the Emperor's Praetorian Guard and the soldiers of the imperial legions. As a Centurion, even a retired one, Valens was still their nominal superior, though the Praetorians would only begrudgingly acknowledge it.

    Valens took the folded message, which bore a wax seal he did not recognize; however, there was no mistaking who it originated from. Without opening it, he nodded to the men, who each rendered a quick salute before riding away towards Rome.

"You will find what you seek on the road back to Rome!" one of the riders shouted over his shoulder. "We'll keep the road quiet for the time you need." Valens snorted at the remark.

"Bastards must be keeping a close watch on me if they knew where to find me," he mused as he looked down at the message. He sighed and walked over to the nearest tree, sat down, and broke the seal. He swallowed hard when he read the contents therein, although he knew it had only been a matter of time before his services were called for again.

My dearest Conqueror of Britannia!
I have a trifling task for you, one that will not be too much of a bother.
There is a Judean named Mathias of Joppa who stole a silver pitcher and goblet set from my establishment. I want these returned and Mathias punished. You need not kill him; however, he must be taught a painful lesson.
Your wife has agreed to be my guest for the next few days. Please come and join us as soon as you have completed your task.
Me fein do anam

He had grown to hate the Empress' cryptic speech. He still did not know what *me fein do anam* meant, or even what language it was. He grimaced at the implications of Svetlana staying with her. His wife was a pseudo-hostage who would be taken as the Empress' 'guest' any time she needed him to complete a vile task for her. Messalina was clever enough to know that should Valens decide to forsake his family's ring, he would never abandon his wife. He shrugged and figured there was nothing to do but punish a thief.

Valens found a small copse of trees at the base of a small hill that jutted back from a bend in the road. He climbed the short rise, which gave him an excellent view of the road and traffic. The Empress' message had described the cart that Mathias was riding in. Since most of the wheeled traffic moved in and out of Rome at night, there were but few pedestrians and some farm carts utilizing the road during the peak of the day, and he knew the Praetorians would delay any traffic that may be following the Judean. At length, he saw a small cart carrying bearing hay, drawn by a pair of oxen. The lone driver was stooped low behind the reigns, his hooded cloak covering his head despite the heat of the sun. Valens verified that there were no other carts or people within earshot; clearly Mathias was trying to avoid being seen. The Centurion gave a mirthless laugh, for the Judean was clearly an amateur at being inconspicuous.

He stepped out into the path of the slow-moving cart, keeping his weapon concealed. The Judean pulled his cart to a stop, keeping a wary distance from the Centurion.

"Mathias of Joppa?" Valens asked casually.

"Who wants to know?" Mathias replied, placing a hand on a spatha cavalry sword that sat on the bench next to him.

"A friend," Valens replied. "Well, a potential client anyway. You have something that I want."

"And what could a poor farmer like me have that a legionary officer could possibly want?" The question threw Valens, but he then realized that he was wearing his Centurion's belt and he cursed himself for such an amateurish mistake.

"I hear you're a purveyor of fine silver," he replied, deciding to use a more direct approach, since his status as a Roman soldier was now compromised. He produced the leather coin pouch that still held his payment for killing the merchant's son.

"I may have acquired a few items in my time that I'd be willing to offload for the right price. What are you looking for?"

"A goblet and pitcher set," Valens answered. He watched Mathias swallow hard and he immediately tried to mentally disarm him. "My wife has a passion for silver, yet has not been able to find a goblet set to her liking. You wouldn't happen to have come across such a thing, have you?"

Mathias grinned in reply and started to reach for a sack that lay behind the seat. He then threw it at Valens before drawing his sword. Despite his age, Valens had lost none of his reflexive speed. He caught the heavy sack and tossed it aside as Mathias fell on him. The Judean's momentum proved to be his undoing and Valens used it to throw him to his back; his sword flying from his hand. In a flash, the centurion drew his gladius and thrust the point to within an inch of the Judean's throat.

"That wasn't very nice!" Valens chastised. He slammed the pommel of his weapon into the man's head, knocking him senseless momentarily. He then stood and kicked the Judean's weapon away before opening the sack and dumping its contents onto the ground. There were numerous valuables to include plates, candelabras, jewellery, and a pitcher and goblet set that Valens could only assume came from the Empress Messalina.

"You're no poor farmer," he muttered, "You're a bloody thief!"

"Please," Mathias pleaded, "I only took from those who would not miss what was taken! The...the harvest was poor last year and my family was starving!"

"You're as poor of a liar as you are at being inconspicuous," Valens retorted. "I doubt that you have a family, much less that you are poor and starving. The destitute do not wield military issued weapons! Who did you steal this from, eh?"

"No one that would miss it," Mathias replied, swallowing hard.

"Oh, so you're a murderer too."

"No!" the Judean shouted quickly. "No, I mean he was already dead when I found it!" Valens sneered as he picked up the spatha and turned it over in his hands.

"Gerizim," Valens said quietly. Out of the corner of his eye he saw Mathias' face twitch.

"Wh...what are you talking about?"

"Mount Gerizim, outside of Jerusalem," Valens replied coldly, facing the cowering Judean. "A battle took place there seven years ago. A single cohort of legionaries and a regiment of Samaritan cavalry defeated more than three thousand armed thugs inciting rebellion." He walked slowly towards Mathias, who was sweating in fear. "You were there, weren't you?"

"N...no, I swear I never took up arms against Rome!"

"I never said you did," Valens replied, pointing the tip of the spatha at the terrified man. "You are one of the vilest of creatures; one who robs the corpses of the slain following a battle. At least those we fought were man enough to choose their side and stand their ground for a time! But you are no real man; instead you skulked behind the rocks, waiting to see which side would claim the field. And as we pursued our defeated foe, you and the other vermin crept onto the field to take what you have no right to wield."

"Like I said," Mathias growled, "it was not something that would be missed!" Valens set the sword down and held up the pitcher and a goblet.

"Someone did miss these."

"That vile bitch," Mathias swore under his breath. He then said aloud, "I told you; my…my children were starving, what was I to do?"

"Steal food perhaps," Valens replied, "one cannot eat silver." His tone showed that he knew the Judean was continuing to lie to him. He then walked quickly back to where Mathias lay and knelt on his arm, gladius ready to strike. "As you well know, in the east the penalty for stealing is to cut off the thief's hand."

"No!" Mathias screamed. "Please, I beg you! Not my hand!"

"Then your head perhaps," the Centurion leered, placing the ever-sharp blade against the man's neck. He let the cold steel rest against the Judean's neck, until a sudden stench told him that the man had defecated in his trousers.

"You're not worth killing," Valens spat as he stood over the Judean, who was in a state of panic and shame. He stood and turned away, tossing all the valuables into the sack, which he then hoisted to his shoulder and tossed it onto the cart. As he turned the cart around he could feel the Judean's eyes bore into him.

"Wait!" Mathias cried out. "You cannot take my cart from me…and the silver! I have a delivery to make or else I'm a dead man!"

"You were a dead man the moment you chose this life," Valens retorted over his shoulder. His ears pricked up as he heard the sound of metal scraping against a rock. He dropped to his knees just as the blade of the Judean's sword swung to decapitate him, embedding itself in the cart. Having missed his prey, Mathias was thrown off balance. The Centurion spun around and leapt to his feet, smashing his fist into the man's face. He drew his gladius as the Judean fell to the earth, his weapon stuck in the back of the cart. Valens stepped hard onto his forearm and brought his gladius down in a hard slash, chopping through the man's wrist.

The Judean let out a howl of shock and horrific pain as Valens picked up the still twitching severed hand.

"Tourniquet that arm before you bleed to death," he said casually as retrieved the spatha, climbed into the cart, and rode away. He was nearly a mile from the scene before the Judean's screams stopped echoing in his ears.

There was no guilt associated with this task. He truly hated battlefield looters as the lowest form of life. An enemy who took up arms against him he could respect, but those who only waited until the corpses piled up to steal from those who could no longer defend themselves? Such cowardice was beyond revulsion. It was then Valens realized that there were depths that he could never stoop to. He also understood that continuing in the Empress' 'service' was a sure path to personal damnation. How long would it be before he could justify becoming a battlefield grave robber like Mathias of Joppa?

Chapter X: Imperial Treachery
***

It was maddening having to wait, but Valens knew he had no choice. The Empress had specified the hour which she would send for him. It was well past midnight and still he waited. The servants he had dismissed for the night and he knew Svetlana was still with the Empress, so he waited alone. He felt stifled inside the house, despite its vast open feel; so he settled for waiting on the grass near the gate, which he left half open. As he lay half asleep the light of torches caught his attention. A litter came into sight, carried by a dozen slaves. Numerous cloaked figures that Valens knew to be Praetorians lurked in the shadows along the road. The curtain of the litter was pulled back and Cornelius looked out.

"It is time," he said coldly.

They rode in silence for some time. Valens hated litters. Numerous slaves walking on cobblestones make for an uneven ride. The fact that he could not see where they were going made the ride nauseating; and though neither he nor Cornelius were in the mood for conversation, he needed something to take his mind of the tedious journey.

"The man I punished today was a battlefield grave robber," Valens said.

"Are you trying to justify your actions to me, or to yourself?" Cornelius replied flatly.

"He was at Gerizim," Valens persisted. Even the name of the last place they had served in battle together could not elicit a trace of emotion from Cornelius. "He had with him a spatha that was taken from the body of one of our auxiliary cavalrymen. Though we never had any love for the Samaritans, you know as well as I that there is no lesser form of life than one who steals from those who die in battle!"

"His body was found this afternoon," Cornelius remarked. "Either he went into shock after you cut his hand off, or he did not know how to make a simple tourniquet. But tell me, would you have punished him, knowing what he was, were you not doing Messalina's bidding?" Valens hung his head and breathed deeply through his nose. He had tried to make his actions against the Judean justifiable, yet the Praetorian had taken that with mention of the Empress. He did not answer the question.

"I don't know how much longer I can do this, Cornelius," he said quietly.

"You've chosen your path Valens," the Praetorian Centurion replied, no trace of emotion in his voice. "You should have listened to me on that first night in the brothel. I gave you another chance to leave even before her first summons. You've always been a bit thick-headed, Valens. A pity you've always had to learn your life's lessons the hard way."

"I accept the hardship that comes from whatever lessons I have had to learn," Valens replied. "I only pray that this next one my wife does not have to learn for me."

"Darling!" Svetlana said gleefully she waved to him from a nearby couch. Clearly the Emperor was away from Rome; otherwise Messalina would never have brought them to the imperial palace. Valens leaned over and held his wife close. Whatever his crimes, his personal failings, he knew he could not allow himself to fail her. Their closest friends had always said Svetlana was the female incarnation of Valens, yet he now knew that was a farce. Svetlana was blessed to be devoid of the sickening darkness that crept into the depths of Valens' soul. It was she who had kept the black from swallowing him up all these years.

"What's the matter, love?" she asked, looking up into his worried face.

"Nothing," he lied, shaking his head. "Just a little tired is all. I was out performing a task for the Empress."

"Yes, she told me she had asked a small favour of you," Svetlana observed. "Nothing too difficult, I hope. She's been a wonderful host! I cannot tell you enough how much I've enjoyed her company…still…" her voice trailed off for a minute.

"Yes?" Valens asked.

"Valens," Svetlana said, her face suddenly full of worry, "there's something sinister going on here, isn't there? In the blackened corners of my mind, I swear I can hear the Empress' voice saying things; dark and terrible things. I thought it was but a nightmare."

"That it is," Valens said quietly into his wife's ear. "And it is one I hope we can wake from soon." Svetlana's face showed that she was scared, something that was almost impossible for her. Never had she felt powerless in the face of any adversary until now.

"Stay strong, my love," he said quickly. "I promise I will not leave here without you." The door to the back of the suite was suddenly flung open and the Empress walked in.

"There you are!" she said with a broad smile. "Come, we have a few things to discuss."

"Valens?" Svetlana asked; her face traced with worry. Messalina turned and faced her.

"Oh don't worry, my dear. We'll be but a minute." She smiled sweetly as she and Valens walked to the back room. As soon as the doors closed, her smile turned to a glower of rage and she slapped him hard. *"What have you been telling her?"*

"I didn't have to tell her anything!" the Centurion retorted, unflinching. "You spew forth at the mouth enough that even when intoxicated she was bound to pick up enough to guess your wicked intentions." Messalina turned away from him and paced the room quietly. He then hoped to try and reason with her.

"My lady," he said, "I don't think I can do this anymore." He immediately realized that reasoning with Empress Messalina was an exercise in futility. She spun to face him, her eyes blackened and her face snarling in rage.

"Oh no, no, no!" she snapped. "You do not get off that easily, my love! Just now when you've started to make yourself useful, you think you can just shove off and leave? I don't think so!"

"Look, it was because of your reckless tongue that Svetlana knows!" His words struck a chord with Messalina. She had to see the added risk now that his wife suspected what was happening. And what all *had* she heard the Empress say?

"Very well," she said. Her voice was hard, but her face was no longer a torrent of anger. That she could go to emotional extremes in a flash was enough to make Valens' head swim. "Complete one last task for me, and I shall grant you your freedom."

"Freedom?" Valens said bitterly. "You talk as if I'm a slave."

"When one does what they are told to do, whether they wish to or not, what else does that make them?" The words bit hard into Valens, yet he knew there was no point in arguing them. He then shook his head.

"No, this ends now!" His conviction evaporated as Messalina produced his family ring from the folds of her stola.

"I suppose I will just have to keep this then," she said with a voice full of sarcasm. "Pity, I was almost inclined to give it back to you." Valens closed his eyes and swallowed hard.

"Very well," he said. "One last time, I will do your bidding. You will then give me back my ring and I will take my wife and leave this place."

"You are not in a position to demand anything," Messalina replied coolly. "Complete the task I have for you and if I am feeling generous, I may give you back your ring. As for your wife, I will let you know if I decide to keep her for my own." Her wicked smile caused Valens to snap.

"You will not hold my wife hostage!" he growled. "Either she comes with me, or no deal!"

"Oh, very well," the Empress replied with a bored sigh. "She was rather fun, though. I will have to get my fill of her while you complete your mission. If you survive, then you will be free to take her and leave."

"I did not spend three decades in the legions only to fall foul to a little girl's deception," Valens growled. Messalina laughed at the insult.

"So full of venom," she observed. "I rather like it. Too bad we couldn't have stayed friends." Her brief pouting was deliberately phony and it only served to make Valens' blood boil. Messalina then gave a sinister laugh.

"Now to your mission," she said, becoming serious once more. "You are to break into the home of my step-daughter…and kill Pompey Magnus." Valens exhaled audibly at the directive.

"Pompey Magnus is the descendant of the great Triumvir!" Valens protested. "He is also your son-in-law, who proclaimed to the Senate that Britannia had been conquered…"

"…and who now stands as a direct threat to my own son," Messalina interrupted. "Let me be clear, *Centurion*. Britannicus *will* become Emperor once that old codger, Claudius, mercifully leaves us. The last of the Triumvir's line will not stand in my way!"

"Why not have Cornelius do this one? Or hire some thugs from one of the street gangs?"

"Street thugs are sloppy, do shoddy work; and besides, they would have little chance of breaking into my dear Antonia's home," the Empress remarked. "As for Cornelius; I already told you, you silly man, why I cannot use the Praetorians. And why would I risk losing my most powerful bodyguard? No, I need someone who is not only a professional killer, but one who is also expendable." Messalina laughed once more as Valens glared at her. "Yes my dear, you *are* expendable; you always have been. From the day your daddy left you at the recruit depot, through all those years of bleeding in gods forsaken frontiers, and even now in your retirement, you are but a disposable asset."

"And what of Svetlana?" he asked after a brief pause, fearing the answer.

"She will stay here as my honoured guest," Messalina replied, her wicked grin twisting into a sneer. She glanced over her shoulder and two bare-chested men walked in. They were enormous; one was a black African, the other a German. Each looked to be a full head taller than Valens, with muscles carved out of stone.

"Who the fuck are they?" Valens asked.

"A little added insurance," the Empress replied. "You need not worry. Do my bidding and your wife will not be harmed; for only I will play with her. She has become rather fond of my touch and could use it after the bad dreams the poor thing has had." She ran a fingernail over her lips seductively as she spoke.

"Should you fail me…" Messalina's words trailed off as she looked back at the pair of titans, who each stood with their arms folded across their chest. Their grins of defiance dared the Centurion to fail his mission.

Chapter XI: Lost and Redeemed
***

It was well after midnight the next night as Valens crept along the outer wall that led into the home of Pompey and Antonia. He had spent the day scouting around their residence and formulating a plan. Decades of facing men on the battlefield, and now he was reduced to committing murder for the Emperor's brat of a wife; worse was that he was being tasked with killing the Emperor's own son-in-law!

"Quite the mess you got yourself into, dumbass," he uttered under his breath. He then proceeded to talk to himself as he uncoiled a rope and grappling hook, which he threw over the wall. "Was she worth it? Svetlana seemed to think so, right up until she found out her husband is now a hired killer, tasked with murdering the Emperor's son-in-law! Of course, all she has to do is lie back and let that wicked bitch tongue her twat some more…still, she does have quite the talented tongue." His mind raced more quickly as he ranted in a vulgar monologue to himself.

"And after all, who can say they've actually had sex with an Empress? Oh wait, in this city that's not exactly an achievement! There's rumour that while we were in Britannia she competed against renowned whore to see who could go through the most lovers in a day…and won! How it is that she's only spawned a pair of brats instead of a whole litter is beyond me."

He continued his rambling and self-argument as he climbed onto the wall. There was a window directly across from where he sat, but it looked too small for him to climb through. Instead, he opted for sending his grappling hook up to the roof and proceeded to climb once more. It was only a short distance and he was grateful that the legions had kept him reasonably fit all these years. As he crawled around the rooftop, he found a skylight the led into their bathing chamber. It was perfect, as it would surely be unoccupied at this late hour.

He hooked the rope to the trap door on the skylight and lowered himself down. Inadvertently, his mind jumped back to a time many years before, when he and the legionary squad he was a part of had snuck into an estate in similar fashion. Only difference was they had been on a rescue mission to save the domina who was being held hostage by renegades who had survived the Sacrovir Revolt. For their success, they had been lauded as heroes. And now Valens was feeling anything but heroic.

It was impossible to clear his mind of the constant conflict as he crept along the wall and cracked open the door that led into a hallway. The house was quite large and he had no idea where the master bedroom was; though he surmised it was on the second floor. As the daughter of the Emperor, Valens figured she and her husband would be well guarded. He was therefore surprised to see but a single figure standing outside what he guessed was their room. A dozen Praetorians guarded the outside of the house, but this looked to be a private bodyguard, rather than a professional soldier. The man was leaning against his spear and in the faint light of a single oil lamp he looked to be half asleep. Valens quietly drew his gladius and crept along the wall, keeping to the shadows. When he was but a few feet away he lunged forward and smashed the pommel of his weapon against the side of the man's head. The bodyguard let out a groan as his eyes rolled back into his head. His spear fell to the ground with a loud clatter as he slumped against the wall, out cold.

Valens cursed the echo of the clamour he had caused. He grabbed the oil lamp and rushed into the room. The only other light was the faint glow of the moon, but he could make out the shuffling of bodies as they tried to rouse themselves out of bed.

"What in Juno's name…" he heard Pompey say in a groggy voice which was cut short when the young senator saw the glint of Valens' blade. "So the bitch has sent her assassins for me." Antonia fell protectively over her husband as Valens walked slowly towards them.

"Get away from him!" she screamed. The house was large and Valens then wondered if her voice would carry through all the walls and alert the Praetorians. No doubt it had roused her servants, who would find the Guardsmen. He had to act quickly if he was going to complete his mission and escape. The Praetorians who guarded Pompey and Antonia were not under the influence of Messalina. Even if they were, this was one mission she had left them oblivious to.

"It's alright, my love," Pompey said calmly as he gently pushed his wife off him. "We both knew this day would come." Despite his wife's protesting sobs, he then stood and faced Valens and bared his chest to him. "Do what you must."

It was then that the Centurion was tormented with indecision. In all his years in the legions, whenever he had been required to kill it had been to eliminate Rome's many enemies. The thugs he had slain at Messalina's bidding would not be missed. This man, on the other hand, was not only blameless of any crime; he was a senator and the Emperor's son-in-law! Suddenly his resolve left him and he threw his sword to the floor with a clatter.

"No," he said quietly. "I only kill the enemies of Rome. If the Empress wishes to dispose of me, let her do so." As he spoke, the sounds of heavy footsteps echoed down the hall. Pompey snatched the lamp from Valens and shoved him into the shadows. He then rushed outside and the Centurion heard him talking with a group of Praetorians.

"Everything alright, sir?"

"Fine, no worries. My wife was having a bad dream. I thank you for your vigilance; now return to your posts."

"Yes, sir."

Valens face betrayed his astonishment as Pompey walked back into the room.

"You could have handed me over to them," he noted. "Why didn't you?"

"You are the victim of the Empress," Pompey replied. "You are also a hero of Rome, and I would hate for you to spend your days of retirement awaiting execution."

"Believe me, I am no hero," Valens lamented. "I am a fraud. I let a wicked little girl get the best of me; how pathetic is that?"

"Messalina has undone many," Antonia spoke up, "to include a number of prominent senators."

"We may be able to help you," Pompey remarked.

"How?" Valens asked.

"Even the Empress doesn't know all the ways in and out of the palace," Antonia replied with a grin.

The false panel slid aside and Antonia led Valens into what appeared to be an ornate office, though it was difficult to see with so little light.

"This is my father's study," Antonia said in a low voice. "There is a second passage we must follow to get to Messalina's private wing, where your wife is being held." Though Valens stumbled around in the dark, Antonia seemed to know exactly where everything was. He heard the scraping of stone as the Emperor's daughter slid open the entrance to another secret passage. Inside was completely black. He tried to keep up with Antonia as she quickly walked through the darkness. At length, he found the end of the passage by running into the wall. He gritted his teeth and clutched his forehead as he fought against yelling out loud.

"Here we are," Antonia said as she carefully slid open a stone tile that was only about waist high. A faint glow of lamp light entered the passage. Valens knelt and looked into what appeared to be a secluded hallway. "The room where your wife is being held is just around the far corner to the right. You won't have to worry about the Praetorians; only Messalina's German and African slaves are ever seen here. Even Cornelius is never allowed into this part of the palace."

"Thank you for all you've done," Valens replied. "And to think I was close to killing your husband."

"You love your wife," Antonia reasoned. "You would do anything to get her back. And I daresay that will involve more killing. Are you sure you can handle the Empress' slaves? They are awfully big men!"

"They are also amateurs," Valens remarked with a sinister grin. "I've dispatched far more worthy opponents than them. What of Messalina?"

"She will be at her private brothel tonight," Antonia answered. "I can take you no further. Gods be with you, Centurion Valens."

"And with you," Valens replied. "I do not envy you or your husband's position and I think you will need the help of the divines in the coming years far more than me."

He crept into the hallway without waiting to see Antonia's reaction. He heard the panel being slid closed behind him and knew that he and Svetlana would have to find their own way out of the palace. He reasoned that once he killed the two slaves, no one besides the Empress would even know who he and Svetlana were and he suspected they could probably simply walk out of the palace. It was amazing how easy one could hide in plain sight! He took a deep breath and drew his gladius. The time for stealth was over. As he rounded the corner, the two giants were at first surprised to see him. They then grinned in contempt as Valens walked casually towards them, his gladius drawn.

"Out of my way," he growled through gritted teeth.

"Oh no," the German replied with a shake of his head. The African carried a large club, which he was slapping against the palm of his left hand. "We're going to break your legs, and then make you watch as we fuck your wife. She's of healthy stock, and I have to say I am looking forward to violating every hole of her body."

Valens closed his eyes and breathed deeply through his nose. Instinct, decades of training, and the experience of countless battles would take over now. He did not have a shield or his armour, but he would not need them. He had his gladius, and as big as these men were, they were still amateurs. The African stepped forward and swung his club down in a hard smash. Valens stepped back and then quickly lunged in, punching the man hard on the jaw with his free hand. As the African staggered, Valens plunged his gladius into his throat. He did not want to give the man a chance to scream and he relished as the giant fell to his knees, body convulsing as torrents of blood spurted from his throat and out of his mouth. His eyes rolled into the back of his head and he fell to the ground as Valens wrenched his weapon free. The German's eyes were wide in terror as the Centurion growled at him in rage. As he was unarmed, the German turned to run. Valens quickly jumped onto his back, held a hand over his mouth, and ran his gladius hard across the wicked man's throat. He kept a tight grip over the German's mouth, muffling attempted screams as he sawed away on his throat with contemptuous rage.

As pooling blood gushed onto the floor tiles, he rapidly searched the bodies and found the key that opened the back room. He entered to find Svetlana now lucid and terrified. She leapt up from the bed and threw her arms around him.

"I thought I would never see you again!" she said as he held her close.

"Come on," he replied, taking her by the hand, "We have to get out of here."

As they raced towards the end of the corridor that opened onto the outer wall, a squad of Praetorians suddenly swarmed them.

Valens drew his weapon and backed towards the nearest wall, keeping Svetlana behind him.

"Come on you bastards!" he shouted as his face twisted in rage. "You will not take me or my wife without a lot of pain!"

"We're not here to hurt you, sir!" one of the Guardsmen said quickly.

"What then?" Valens growled. "Are you here to send us back to your mistress, the whorish Empress of Death?" Anger and panic overwhelmed him as Cornelius stepped into the light. Valens gritted his teeth, though the Praetorian Centurion's face betrayed no emotion at all.

"Stand down," Cornelius ordered his men. He then reached into his hip pouch and produced a gold ring. "I didn't think you would want to leave without this." His face was still expressionless as he handed Valens his family ring. The Centurion quickly snatched it from him and stood dumbfounded for a moment.

"You take an awful risk doing this, Cornelius," Valens said, still perplexed.

"I'll be fine," the Praetorian asserted. "Now take your wife and leave this place. My men will escort you and give you safe passage out of the city. I advise you never to return to Rome so long as the Empress Messalina lives."

The faint glow of the predawn gave just enough light for Valens and Svetlana to find their way. Erin and their other servants waited for them by a covered wagon that was tethered to a pair of oxen. Erin had been prompt about packing her master and mistress' belongings. Svetlana's brother, Oleg, was waiting for them as well.

"Everything sorted out?" he asked casually.

"Yes," Valens replied with a genuine smile of relief. "It was just a minor issue is all." His brother-in-law snorted and shook his head.

"Valens, in all the years I've known you, nothing has ever been a 'minor issue' with you," Oleg observed.

"Well at least it was nothing that we couldn't handle." He looked over at his wife and squeezed her hand. She smiled and gently caressed his arm. Svetlana was one of the strongest women he had ever known, and she looked as if she was none the worse for wear. Oleg knew his sister all-too-well and figured there wasn't anything the world could throw at her that she couldn't handle.

"You'll be on your way then," he noted. Valens nodded as Svetlana embraced her brother and kissed him on the cheek.

"Tell Hansi I am sorry we could not wait for him to see us off," she said as she released Oleg. Their brother was making his way south and was expected in Rome in two weeks' time.

"He'll understand," the Norseman replied. "Neither you nor either of our brothers have ever lived what one would call a quiet existence." Svetlana smiled knowingly, held her brother close one last time and then joined Valens in the wagon.

Valens took in a deep breath as they left Ostia behind. The sun dawned and he allowed himself to enjoy its growing warmth. All that had happened over the past few days seemed surreal to him; indeed, he found himself already questioning whether or not it did really happen. Had it all been a nightmare induced by opiate-laced wine? Somehow, he knew that Svetlana would never mention the events surrounding their short stint in Rome. How close had they both come to the abyss? It mattered not. They had survived and as they passed the farm fields and vineyards that lined to road, they looked forward to opening a new chapter in their lives. The career of Centurion Tiberius Valens had ended as volatile as it had begun, and he had faced down an enemy far more dangerous than even the most battle-hardened enemy warriors.

○

"Pompey Magnus still lives," Messalina observed with a bored sigh.

"I'm afraid so," Cornelius replied. "I suspect Centurion Valens had a change of heart at the last."

"He spends his entire life killing, what would have been one more, especially at his Empress' bidding!" Though Messalina was unhappy that Pompey Magnus still lived, there was a coy smile on her face; as if she somehow admired what Valens had done.

"Too bad my gladiators decided to steal his ring from me and pawn it," the Empress remarked, giving Cornelius a knowing look. The ring had disappeared and though Messalina knew the truth, she pretended to accept the Praetorian's explanation.

"A pity indeed," the Praetorian agreed. "Still, they have paid for their crimes with their lives." His face remained stoic, though Messalina knew he lied. The truth was she needed Cornelius and if she were to bring about his downfall for this treachery, it would cause her more trouble than it was worth. In fact, Messalina was not at all sure if she *could* bring down Cornelius. After all, he had been one of the Praetorians who handed Claudius the imperial throne in the first place.

"Hmm, well I shall know better in the future as to whom I can and cannot trust." If Messalina's words unnerved Cornelius, he did not show it. The last three years of his hateful task serving as her bodyguard had taught him to never betray his emotions. Though the Empress Messalina lacked the intelligence, nobility, and sense of duty that Empress Livia Augusta had possessed, she was no less determined when she saw an enemy that needed disposing of. Cornelius assessed that Valens' actions had bought Pompey Magnus a little time, but nothing more.

"Centurion Valens may have outwitted me," the Empress said, correctly guessing his thoughts. She stood with her arms folded across her chest and gazed over the hills to where the rising sun was casting its glow. "But it will not happen again. Even if I have to make a pact with hell and oblivion, I *always* get what I want."

As the Empress walked away, Cornelius knew that this round of their epic game was now over. Valens was a friend and a fellow brother-in-arms; it had been his duty to help him. Had it been anyone else caught up in Messalina's web, he would not have been as willing to risk his career, not to mention his life. It was a fascinating and deadly game that he and the Empress played against each other. Everyone else was but an unwitting pawn, even Claudius himself.

"You have already made your pact with hell and oblivion," he said quietly as he watched the Empress walk away, his eyes filling with hate. His hand gripped the pommel of his gladius as he glared at her. "The time will come when the thirst of my blade will be sated on your pretty little neck."

Epilogue: Four Years Later
The Gardens of Lucullus

The Death of Valerian Messalina, by Victor Biennoury

How did it come to this? Messalina asked herself.

She had waited years for this moment; the time had come to depose that old fool Claudius and place her lover, Gaius Silius, on the imperial throne. She had committed herself to a relationship with Silius, a senator whose father of the same name had served with great renown during the Germanic Wars and the Sacrovir Revolt. A mercy that the old legate was long dead; how would he react, with the knowledge that his son was guilty of high treason?

Messalina and the younger Silius had been lovers for some time. At her behest, he had divorced his wife, and now she promised him the imperial throne. She had disposed of her most ardent rivals within the Senate. Whether through deception or brute force, she had eliminated virtually every potential rival. Even Pompey Magnus had only been given a brief reprieve when that bastard Centurion Valens had balked at killing the last descendant of the famous Triumvir. In the end, Messalina had managed to have him killed when he was secretly in bed with a male prostitute in her employ. With Claudia Antonia married off to Messalina's half-brother, the only rival left to her was Claudius himself. The young and virile Silius would make a far more suitable Emperor.

Their marriage was known to all in Rome except the Emperor. The old fool was in Ostia, and by the time he returned he would be deposed and Silius would be Caesar…or so Messalina thought.

Claudius' freedmen had gotten word of the plot and had warned the Emperor. And despite the number of large bribes paid, the men of the Praetorian Guard had proven loyal to Claudius. During the drunken celebrations that followed Messalina's 'marriage' to Silius, the large contingent of soldiers bearing down on them were at first assumed to be coming to join in the celebration. Instead, their swords were drawn and they fell upon the villa with a vengeance. Over two hundred guests were arrested, along with Silius. No doubt he would be strangled or crucified for his treason. It was unlikely that Claudius would have all the others killed, though their penalties would be stiff; exile and deprivation would be the fate of many.

As for the Empress herself, she now awaited her fate in the Gardens of Lucullus. She had sent her children with a message to their father, begging him to come to her and forgive her. Britannicus and Octavia were too young to fully comprehend their mother's crimes, and they would implore their father to show mercy. Yet they would not reach their father in time, or at least that was what Messalina assumed when she saw it was not Claudius who entered the gardens. It was only now, when the hour had grown late that Messalina finally realized her intrigues had gone too far and taken her to the edge of oblivion. She had one chance to live, and it had to come soon.

○

Cornelius felt a series of emotions and none of them good. The day he had long prophesized had come and he could at last avenge his beloved Rebekkah. And yet he took no joy in what he was about to do. It was already well after dark when he left the imperial palace, along with a full century of his men. They had walked right past where the Emperor's freedmen held back his children. Octavia was sobbing loudly and Britannicus had cried repeatedly, *"Don't kill my mother! Please don't kill my mother!"*

"If only you knew what your mother was, boy," he had growled under his breath.

He and his men were focused on their task. This was simply a job, nothing more. Cornelius knew that Messalina's mother was with her. They had been estranged for years, yet now she at least took some pity on her daughter at the very end. He hoped there would not be trouble, for Domitia was virtuous and noble woman. She was not to be harmed in any way, but also, she could not be allowed to interfere with their duty.

"Cornelius?" Messalina asked, perplexed. She then sneered at him in defiance. "Did you come with my husband so that you could gloat?" Her mother, Domitia, stepped slowly away, knowing why Cornelius had come. Praetorians fanned out on either side, surrounding the interior of the garden.

"Your husband did not come with me," he replied without emotion. He knew if he let her see that this was a cold duty for him and nothing more, it would add to the gravity of what she would view as an insult.

"What do you want?" she asked quietly, knowing tears forming in her eyes. How could she have thought any different?

"Your life!" he barked, drawing his gladius. The surrounding Praetorians drew their weapons as well. In his left hand, Cornelius held a pugio dagger. "I am to offer you the dagger first; to let you at least end your life with *some* semblance of dignity."

"Dignity?" the accompanying freedman spat. "You do not deserve any *dignity*, you vile whore! You should be slowly strangled, like the traitor Silius! But then that is a mercy for him too, isn't it? After all, having been with you his cock has probably rotted, along with his brain!"

Both Messalina and her mother were in shock that the freedman was allowed to verbally assault her so. It was Domitia who appeared to realize that it was done deliberately. A slave or freedman was not expected to act with decorum. The Praetorians were professionals who would do their job without malice or glee. It was the freedman who was there to insult the Empress at the last. Without a word, Cornelius tossed the dagger to Messalina. It landed in a crash at her feet.

"What...what will happen if I can't?" she asked, fighting against the coming sobs.

"Your head will be chopped off and put on a spike!" the freedman spat. Eyes wide with terror at the implication, she glanced over at Cornelius, who nodded sternly.

"No," she said, shaking her head quickly and backing away. "Not my head!" Her mother quickly stepped forward and picked up the dagger. She looked at it for a moment and then over at Cornelius, who stood stone-faced. She then turned to her daughter and shoved held the dagger up to her.

"Your life is finished," she said coolly. "All that remains is to make a decent end." She then quickly walked away. Praetorians were blocking her exit, but with a nod from Cornelius they let her pass.

Hands trembling uncontrollably, Messalina unsheathed the dagger and held it under her breast. The point of the sharpened weapon terrified her and she could not drive it home.

"Oh, what's the matter, love?" the freedman sneered. "Did the Empress of Death lose her nerve? So easy to play with other people's lives, now isn't it?" She gritted her teeth in anger but could not speak. She knew the man was talking about Pompey Magnus, whose death she had finally arranged the year before. She wanted to lunge over and drive the dagger into the freedman's throat, but Cornelius stood in her way. She looked up at him piteously.

"I can't do it, Cornelius," she sobbed. "I can't do it!"

Without a word, the Praetorian Centurion swung his gladius in a hard swing, the blade driving deep into her neck. The dagger dropped from Messalina's hand and she fell to her knees as another Praetorian stepped in and held her up by her hair. Her eyes were wide and her throat gurgled with blood from the ruptured artery that gushed forth and over her partially severed windpipe. After a moment's pause, while the freedman's laughter echoed in her ears, Cornelius brought his weapon in an even harder slash, cutting the rest of the way through her windpipe, spinal column, and cleaving her entire head from her body. The freedman was immediately silent, his façade complete. Domitia walked back into the garden as the Praetorian dropped her daughter's head next to her body. Cornelius looked at her momentarily and then turned and walked out, his Guardsmen following.

Valens had just risen from an invigorating bath when servants ushered in an imperial messenger. The poor man was shivering and wrapped tightly in his cloak.

"Not used to the northlands, are we?" Valens asked with a grin. The winter wind was howling and even he rarely ventured outside his warm estate this time of year.

"N...no sir," the messenger replied. "Bloody hell but it's cold!" The man then reached into his pouch and presented a scroll.

"Message for Centurion Tiberius Valens," he said, handing a sealed scroll to Valens. The retired Centurion looked at the seal briefly before breaking it and reading the contents of the message. It was very short and he showed no emotion regarding its contents. The setting sun shone through the western windows that overlooked the spectacular view of the mountains. The man who had come all the way from Rome would have enjoyed its view more, were he not frozen to the core.

"It is late," Valens said, looking up. "Servants will take your belongings and show you to one of the guest rooms. Your horse will be placed in my stables. There is a fire in the great hall; I suggest you warm yourself up there. By your quarters is a private bath that you are free to use." He then waved him off.

"Thank you, sir!" Doubtless the man thought he would have to try and find the nearest inn, which was a good hour's ride, in the coming night. Given the contents of the message, Valens felt a little inclined to be a good host to the man who had ridden well over a thousand miles to reach him.

He then called for wine and walked through the double doors that led onto a large balcony. Svetlana was there, relishing in the wind that whipped through her hair. She smiled at her husband as he handed her the message. He then took a chalice of wine from the servant's tray and held another up to Svetlana as she finished reading the short note.

As they looked towards the setting sun that cast its soft glow on the horizon, they faced south in the direction of Rome and raised their chalices in salute. At length Svetlana spoke.

"Queen of the night, she brought eternal dark; now she is gone, the Empress of Death."

Historical Postscript

In the wake of Messalina's execution, her lover, Silius, as well as most of her inner circle were arrested and put to death. Claudius made the Praetorians promise to kill him if he ever married again, yet two years later in January, 49 A.D., he did marry once more. Several candidates vied for the position, including his second wife, Aelia Paetina, the mother of his daughter, Claudia Antonia. Despite rumours that said Claudius and Aelia still had feelings for each other, politics won out and he married his own niece, Agrippina the Younger. Her son, Lucius Domitius Ahenobarbus, would later adopt the name Nero. Nero married his stepsister, Octavia, in 53 A.D. Claudius died in 54 A.D. at the age of sixty-three. Many ancient historians suspect that he was poisoned by Agrippina. Though Claudius had named both Nero and Britannicus as his heirs, as Nero was the elder and Britannicus still underage, it was Nero who became sole Emperor. A year later, Britannicus was murdered on Nero's orders. Nero divorced Octavia in 62 A.D., falsely accused her of adultery, and banished her to a remote island, where she soon died. Whether her death was suicide or murder is unknown.

Claudia Antonia would have as hapless of an end as her half-sister. Messalina would finally succeed in killing her husband, Pompey Magnus. Sources conflict on how and why he was killed, but the result was that Antonia was then married to Messalina's half-brother, Faustus Cornelius Sulla Felix, in 47 A.D. They were married for eleven years, but only had one child, who died before his second birthday. In 58 A.D. Sulla was exiled, and four years later murdered, on the orders of Nero. When Nero's second wife, Poppaea Sabina, died from complications suffered during a miscarriage, Nero attempted to marry Antonia. Her refusal of his advances was the signing of her own death warrant. Nero had her arrested on trumped up charges. Claudia Antonia was executed in 66 A.D. at the age of thirty-six. Her ignominious death ended a great lineage. Claudius' maternal grandparents had been Marc Antony and Octavia, the sister of Augustus; therefore, Antonia's death also brought and end to the lineage of Antony.

Made in the USA
Middletown, DE
17 April 2019